PHASES OF EXISTENCE

AND THINGS I LEARNED WHEN I WAS DEAD

JUSTIN CASE

authorHOUSE®

AuthorHouse™
1663 Liberty Drive
Bloomington, IN 47403
www.authorhouse.com
Phone: 833-262-8899

Published by AuthorHouse 08/12/2020

ISBN: 978-1-7283-6904-4 (sc)
ISBN: 978-1-7283-7044-6 (e)

Print information available on the last page.

Any people depicted in stock imagery provided by Getty Images are models, and such images are being used for illustrative purposes only.
Certain stock imagery © Getty Images.

This book is printed on acid-free paper.

Because of the dynamic nature of the Internet, any web addresses or links contained in this book may have changed since publication and may no longer be valid. The views expressed in this work are solely those of the author and do not necessarily reflect the views of the publisher, and the publisher hereby disclaims any responsibility for them.

CONTENTS

THE END OF ONE IS THE BEGINNING OF ANOTHER.

If someone told you that getting shot four times was the best thing that ever happened to them, you would probably think that they were crazy or maybe that they have had a pretty tough life. In my case, either way is true.

I did get shot four times and it was the best thing that ever happened to me. I definitely had a few rough times in my life and there is no doubt I am probably a little bit crazy as well. However, that is not why it was the best thing that ever happened to me.

I look back on it now and think it is so funny, how I was for such a long time, afraid of the best thing that will ever happen in my life. Now I know death is not a bad thing at all. You will also eventually find out that it is a magnificent transformation. That is, of course, if you did not create a lot of bad karma in your life.

I should have died at least a dozen times because of the all the different things that have occurred in my life. In fact, on a few other occasions, I have had to experience much more pain than just getting shot four times.

I have had some absolutely unbelievable things happen to

me, but I never died; well, maybe I should say I never stayed dead.

I even had my life saved one time by a little bunny rabbit. Yes, you read it right: a little bunny rabbit, or at least I thought at the time it was a bunny rabbit.

Anyway, I was driving to Southern Utah a few years ago. It was getting late and dark. Not too dark to notice how extremely beautiful it is down here. It was dark enough though, to feel the anticipation and excitement to want to hurry up and get there.

I was not trying to turn my car into a time machine or anything like that, well at least not at that time anyway. Betsy, (that was my car then) could go quite fast. She had a 400 big barrel and when I first got her I lost my driver's license for a year for going a little over 120 miles an hour. However, I was not driving like a crazy maniac that day; I did though start to drive a little bit too fast.

I was making my way up a beautiful red rock canyon listening to music with my beautiful companion. She may have been my wife at that time I do not remember. But Lonna was absolutely unforgettable. I must have taken my eyes off the road for a minute, maybe just to glance at her.

We were both in our early twenties. We had been together since she was in high school. She was my first wife and probable the best wife, so far in this life. I will refer to her as #1 because it basically went downhill from her. We loved camping and partying a lot. On the radio we sing, while it plays Van Halen's "I Can't Drive 55." Just for a little motivation. She is getting a little tired and so am I at that point.

She scoots herself over closer to me and then she lays her head on my shoulder.

I love the scent of her hair. She still has that new girl smell. My mind begins to wander off as one of her hairs starts to tickle my nose.

Just then I look back at the road when this rabbit ran right out in front of me. I hit the brakes and yelled out "stupid little bunny!" My sweetie screams right in my ear as I swerved to the left to miss it. The tail end of my 76 Malibu Classic does this little fish tail move. I then realized I am on a hair pin turn that had an unusually steep drop off. I turn into the slide and then my car recovers itself going the right direction in the proper lane.

Wow I am not sure how that turned out right, but it did, and our hearts are pumping like crazy from the adrenaline rush. Falling asleep now while driving was not going to be a concern. I think we both noticed, at the same time, that we may have wetted ourselves a tiny bit.

I then realized if that "stupid" little bunny had not run out in front of me, we would have gone right over that cliff. I know surviving that fall would have been impossible. So essentially that little bunny saved our lives.

I looked in my mirror for that bunny and it was nowhere to be found. There was no bunny, but I did see a girl standing there. She surely seemed to be kind of out of place.

I did not see her before that little mishap, but I did after and I remember the look on her face like it was yesterday. I even thought to myself, she had to have seen the same thing I seen. At that time, I did not give it any more thought. I think it was a few hours later I did think about it, and I said out loud to myself "what the heck was she doing there anyway?"

There was no place for that bunny to go, it just disappeared and then there she was. I believe to this day that was not just a little bunny, I believe it was divine intervention.

That was not the first time I faced death, but it was one of many times I could have died or would have died if I would not have had some kind of supernatural protection. I know how crazy it sounds now and I would have had a tough time believing it if it would not have happened to me personally. In fact, I am sure I went into denial and forgot all about it until much later. Now I know I survived that because of outside influences.

It was not until I was shot four times that I actually did die. I left my body and went to the spirit world and I met my guardian angel.

The spirit world was the most beautiful place I had ever seen. I felt wonderful and I wanted to stay, but it was decided that I could not stay there. I was not given another chance to come back to my body and this life. I was *forced* to come back to this physical life and to this phase of existence. It was not my time yet, and for an exceptionally long time, I was very confused and disappointed.

MOST IMPORTANT MESSAGE

I had a lot of questions about death and God before that happened but when I woke up, I had the answer to everything I ever wondered about. It was like I had my own awakening or an epiphany. The first thing I found out was, and I know this for a fact, without any doubt at all, is that the best thing that will ever happen to you is you will die, that is if you don't create a lot of bad karma for yourself.

If you live right and are generally an honest person, not a saint, but someone who makes good choices and you do not hurt anyone, you will like all of us, have a magnificent transformation into your next phase of existence.

In our physical life we experience much pain and so many challenges that we need to learn from, but when we leave our physical bodies, we leave all our pain and suffering behind.

There are some exceptions such as addictions, personality traits and behaviors that we retain good and bad as well. Such as smoking or drinking, we can still have unquenchable cravings after we leave our physical bodies. Therefore, it is best to try to abandon all unproductive behavior.

I know that if you were born a happy healthy child and

you lived everyday of your life without a single care, happy from sunup to sundown. You never got sick or as much as scratched your finger or shed a single tear.

When you die and shed this body, you will have a magnificent transformation. It is electrifying, exhilarating, liberating, wonderful, magnificent transformation.

It is then that you will know that every day that you were alive in this body, on this Earth, you were suffering in comparison to how you will feel when you die and leave this body.

Then you will advance and have a magnificent transformation into your next phase of existence. Of course, that is if you live a good life you are honest and never hurt anyone.

If you knew how wonderful you will feel when you leave this physical life, you would kill yourself to get there. But do not do that because if you do you may find yourself in a timeless living nightmare. We all need to just tough it out here on Earth. We need to do what is right and let life, or death and our next phase of existence come in its own due time.

I do not have a death wish, I used to be a little bit afraid of death but now I look forward to that day when my life here on Earth ends. I do not have a death wish, but I do look forward to experiencing that magnificent transformation into my next phase of existence. The end of one phase of existence is the beginning of another.

REMEMBERING MY
CHILDHOOD

I guess I had better back up a little and start from the beginning. I was born in 1964 to good hardworking, honest parents. We attended church on a regular basis. My mother was always there for me for whatever I needed.

My father, not so much, he seemed to always be working 2, 3 and 4 jobs at a time to keep a roof over our heads and to see that we never went hungry. I thank God for them and the sacrifices they made for me. I am incredibly lucky to have had them.

I am the youngest of 4 with 1 brother and 2 sisters; for the most part I had a good childhood. One of my childhood memories was how every Christmas morning my siblings would wake me up. Before sunrise, early in the morning and send me in to wake up Mom and Dad.

They pretty much knew that because I was the youngest and the cutest, I might add, that there was no way in heck I could ever get into trouble. I would then wake my parents up and our Christmas would begin.

When I was incredibly young my Dad took my brother and I to get our haircut.

We used to go to this place on the corner of walk and don't walk in Sunset City. Most of the barbers were ok but one of them we called the "hair puller". Every time we would go there one of us would get stuck with him.

There were about 8 barber chairs in two rows facing each other and we would go in, take a number, and sit down. I remember sitting there with my fingers crossed hoping that either I would not get him, or my brother would. It seemed for some crazy reason I always got him.

One of the last times we went there I decided I would just get my head shaved. I am not sure why I did that. I then went home with my head covered with my coat to surprise my Mom. When I first seen her, I pulled my coat off my head I yelled surprise, she positively was.

That was when she started calling me this nickname and it stuck. From that point on I was called this nick name, and every imaginable combination of this nick name you can think of. To this very day most anyone who knows me calls me by that nickname.

MY FIRST EXPERIENCE OF DEATH

I was about six years old when I had one of my first memories of almost dying. I was with my brother visiting my grandparents in Idaho. The rest of my family already left to go back home while we stayed an extra day or two. We boarded a Greyhound bus from St Charles Idaho headed for Sunset City, Utah around noon time.

As soon as I got on the buss I needed to go to the bathroom. It was in the bathroom that I noticed that my urine was red, and it hurt to pee. I went back to sit next to my brother and soon again I had to go. Again, it was red, bloody, and hurt.

I was scared to tell anyone on the bus what was happening and just kept running back to the bathroom. I think it was four or five hours later we finally arrive in Sunset City and I was too week to move and was rushed to the hospital.

I was so low on blood that I almost literally pissed myself to death. I had surgery and when I woke up several hours later, it was in the middle of the night. I woke up and looked around, I could not see anyone. There was nobody around. It was nighttime and I was scared.

So being just a kid not knowing where I was, I started to

cry. A candy striper hears me and comes in. She asked me why I was crying, and I remember telling her I was hungry. "The kitchen is closed now but would you like some crackers and milk?" She asked. She made me feel much better and I went back to sleep.

She was next to my bedside every time I woke up and looked up at her. I survived although doctors said I came awfully close to dying on that bus.

After the surgery they had to put a tube up in me and X-ray me while I was urinating. This was to make sure that it was a successful operation. That hurt so bad and according to my Mom I was extremely pissed off no pun intended.

I was able to recover ok but years later I found out that I could not have kids. I do not know for a fact that it was that incident that made me not able to have kids or if it was just that God knew better than to let me have kids.

Not because I do not like kids or would not be a good father but because of knowing that if I could have kids, I would most likely end up with several hundred of them.

I know I can be a great Dad now and I honestly wish I did have several hundred of them. That becomes kind of my passion later in life when I became face to face with homeless and starving children in the Philippines.

MY FIRST RUN IN WITH THE LAW

Another great memory I had was playing cards with my Mom. Crazy 8's or Go Fish. My Mom never seemed to be too busy to take the time to play with me and that would make me so happy. It was on one of those days that my life would take a drastic turn.

I believe I was about 8 years old when I was robbed of my childhood and life would never be the same. It would change my life dramatically and I would begin down a dreadful pathway of misery, self-destruction, and discontent.

At the time I did not think I deserved it, but I did rub the police the wrong way at a young age. Kids are brutally honest and sometimes that can get you into trouble. I did not do anything to deserve it, but I did become a victim of one of societies ugliest of secrets.

It was a major turning point in my life at that time. I know now as I am remembering my childhood. One day I was playing cards with my Mom and before I even knew it, I was Living up to my nickname.

THE CONFESSION

School was out for the summer and I was enjoying one of those games of cards with my Mom. We lived on a quiet street where all our neighbors knew each other and each other's business. There really was not ever too much action happening around in our neighborhood so whenever police would show up anywhere, that was the direction where everybody had their nose pointed.

Our neighborhood was for the most part one big family and everyone genuinely cared about each other. I believe that was perhaps mostly due to our Christian culture.

As we played cards, I noticed a police car pull up in front of our house. My Mother and I both gasped and said, "I wonder what they could be here for." They made their way up to our front door; one was a Sargent for the Sunset City Police Department. Sargent Pudman, I am eight years old and we already have brutal history with each other.

He lived the next block over and just down from our house. I was probably one of the only kids he even knew around there, and he did not like me or my friends.

The first time I remember meeting him was a year or so earlier my friend Romon and I were walking down the railroad tracks. It was a usual place to run, hide and play.

Weeds grew two times taller that we could see, and we would play war with dirt clods.

I could pull out some long grass with dirt stuck on it and fling it in the air with remarkable accuracy. Splat right in Romon's Ear I hear him yell "YOU BASTARD!" It was a little soggier than most I noticed when I looked back at him. He is chasing me mad for revenge and I am running away trying not to pee my pants from laughing when I trip and fall on my face.

I fell over two enormous greasy toolboxes in the tall grass.

I ran over to them and yelled "Hey Bonehead, look what I found!" He runs over and sure enough I had a lucky find and his anger turns into excitement. They were so big, and we were so little it took us an hour just to drag them home. I found them but I had to share with my Buddy Bonehead. I finally was able to get my toolbox home and when my Dad seen it, he said I had to turn them into the police station.

I was not happy about that and I tried as hard as I could to change his mind, but he would not have it any other way. He was a deputy Sheriff at the time and always said honestly is the best policy.

He takes me and my find to the police station and there he is, Pudman. He told me if nobody claims it in three months then I can have them. Three months later my Dad takes me over to check on it and good old Pudman tells me "Oh we sold them in an auction." I said "What?" He repeated himself and I went crazy and asked him "Ok where is my money? How much did you sell my stuff for?" All I got was "Sorry kid!" "Ya your right Dad, honesty is the best policy!" I yelled.

I cringe when I see him and to this day I am still affected

by his actions. He was the one person I for many years blamed for ruining my life, and as soon as he reached the top step he began to knock.

My Mother answered the door and they asked her if they could talk to me alone. Do not ever do that. If anyone wants to talk to your underage kid alone just say NO! My Mother did not see any harm at the time but if she would have had any idea what they were going to do to me, I am sure she would not have let them talk to me alone. She called me into the room, and they took me outside with them.

They wasted no time at all and put me into hand cuffs and then into the back of their patrol car. I was in tears, as I was only 8 years old.

That is when they told me that if I did not confess to a particular crime, they were going to take me straight to jail and throw away the keys. It was breaking into a junkyard down the street, a crime I did not commit but if I confessed, I could go back inside my house.

I did not know anything about it, but I did not want to go to jail so I confessed.

"You are going to need to talk to the detective in a few days, we will get ahold of you now we know where you live," they said as they walked to their patrol car. I then went back into my house and my mother questioned me about it. I did not know what to say.

I did not want my Dad to find out, so I just said it was nothing. It was a long five days I had to wait to talk to those detectives.

Even more for a kid especially at my age to try to understand what was going on. I had a lot of unanswered questions about what was going to happen to me. I did not want to go to jail. I was very scared about what was going to happen because of the confession.

I believe there are many innocent people behind bars doing time for crimes they did not commit. Just because of police like Pudman, who were lazy and did not want to do their job, did not know how to do their job, or just did not care.

Later, many years after that, I found out that when police are being interviewed, they are given an IQ test and if they score too high on that test, they do not get the job. One reason is because the government does not want to put people through several weeks of basic training just to have them find another job, or a better job. They want to hire people who think they could never find a better job. That is why we have injudicious cops, stupid cops or cops who just do not care. Face it, if they were smarter, they would be lawyers.

I also believe that there are only a couple reasons why people become cops. One is they seriously want to change the world or at least make a difference. Two they were bullied, or they were bullies in school and now they want to be bullies all the time or three, they want to have control over other people. Maybe there are some who want to do good things but once they find out that their efforts are in vein or they cannot do what they want, most just give up and do not care anymore. I am not saying all cops are stupid, but I know that they do not become cops for the money. I know that because one of my Dads jobs was a deputy sheriff.

I know pay is part of the problem, they have a horrendous

job and they should get paid more. I am sure if they did get paid more, we would have better cops.

I do know that the two cops that came to my house that day were stupid, lazy bullies who did not know how to do their jobs and probably also just did not care.

Not all cops, I realize, are like that but these two were. They even looked alike, close enough to be twins. both in tip top shape, for a basketball that is. They totally fit that stereotype of cops that love doughnuts! no kidding, I knew I could outrun them, but I do not know if I could out roll them, especially going downhill. I also let them for many years make my life miserable. I eventually figured out how to take that power back.

Back to my story, I went to talk to the detective about a week later and he asked me "So how did you do it?" I said I didn't know, and he said, "What do you mean you don't know?" I just repeated what I had said the first time, and he said, "You don't know because you didn't do it?"

"Yes," I replied.

He said, "I know you didn't do it because we have the guys that *did* do it and they don't even know who you are." He then asked me "Why did you say that you did it?" I told him "They said if I didn't say I did it, then they were going to take me straight into jail and throw away the keys."

He then told me "Don't ever say you did something that you didn't do." I found out that those two fine officers were reprimanded for what they did to me. I do not know if they got demoted or passed over but from that point on, they made it a point, to make my life miserable.

Those two cops in the Sunset City Police Department

harassed me, bullied me, and got other kids to bully me in school until I decided to just drop out of school and society. I went underground as much as much as possible to avoid getting hurt and harassed all the time. I was targeted, patted down, and ripped off every day they seen me.

If I had anything of value, they took it. I was thrown in detention so many times I forgot the count. One time they took my backpack because it had new DVDs in it, and they said that they looked stolen. I spent 4 days for that before they finally decided not to file charges on me, and I never got my stuff back.

Juvie is not too bad once you get used to it. You never have a minute of privacy. The food is all made of powder. Powder eggs, powder milk, powder pan cakes, I'm surprised they did not give us powdered water too.

It is hard at first to get used to how the echo of kids screaming at each other and at the guards makes your ears ring. The sounds in juvie like steel doors slamming shut send shuttering vibrations through you all the way down to your bones.

Everyone staring at you and asking why you in there. You can only see the girls when lining up in the hallway for meals. Impossible to pick up chicks! I do not think it is ok for kids to have to get used to being locked up at all, but you do get used to it.

When I got old enough to drive, they impounded my car. They turned the entire police force against me, so needless to say I grew up hating police. You can just imagine what that did for my decaying relationship with my father. I believe that kids should grow up knowing that police are good people.

They should believe that they can trust them and believe that police are there to help and protect them.

It is a shame that I grew up afraid of cops and at a relatively early age, fear turned into hatred. This was in the 80's and it is an unbelievable shame that we now in 2020 are still having nationwide protests for Police Brutality.

It is a total shame that the people who are supposed to be there to protect you, not to abuse and kill you. From Rodey King to Paul George and all other lives senselessly destroyed for nothing other than racism.

I am so sorry for this divide and want to help but what can one man do? The power of one is stronger than you think. Is it wrong to say that all lives matter? Not if you sincerely believe it. Historically the U.S. does not have a great record for treating people of color. I hope we all live to see the day that skin color makes no difference.

Let us spread hope for the future don't dwell in the past but take it one day at a time is the best way to last.

I look back at my life now and I realize that the more I was focused on inanimate objects the more unhappy I became starting with those tools I found. Maybe because I was never satisfied with what I had.

Now I do not really care about that stuff I am a whole lot happier person.

THANKS FOR THE CHOCOLATES

It should be obvious that growing up I hated cops, but I felt that I had plenty reason for that at that time. It was not long after those two cops got reprimanded for what they did to me that I began to notice a pattern of harassment from them. I started having confrontations first on a weekly basis and it grew consistently into an everyday thing.

A few things stand out from my past like once when I was in 7th grade I was walking home from school, and out of nowhere a bully Derk the jerk steps up to me, knocks my books out of my hands and then punches me in the face for no apparent reason. When he walked away and I started picking up my stuff I noticed those two cops sitting in their patrol car, and then laughing as they drove by.

Another time a similar incident happened only I was walking home from school on Valentine's Day with a heart shaped box of chocolates in my hand. I got them from my first girlfriend, Kelly Tanner. She was noticeably short and cute. I was so happy and then suddenly, some kid walked up to me and grabbed the candy and punched me right in the eye.

As he walked away, he happened to say, "Hey nothing

personal." I didn't quite know what he meant by that at the time, I was upset then, but I continued walking home and a minute later there they were again parked on the side of the road, the same two cops. As I walked by one of them said "Nice shiner," referring to my newly acquired black eye as he placed a piece of candy in his mouth. Then the other one said, "Thanks for the chocolates," they both laughed, as I walked away.

I got the feeling that they were punishing me because I got them into trouble, and it was not going stop for a while.

That is when I started calling cops, "pigs." I had no idea that I started a tornado of abuse when I spouted of in the police station about my tools. Or maybe I did not tell their boss the proper lie when they framed me. I was a target and it was not going to stop anytime soon.

Those cops did everything possible to make my life a living hell and it was not just them, as I said earlier one of them was a sergeant and he turned the entire police force against me.

I believe that he spread the word that I was some kind of enemy to the force. I do not now what he told all the other pigs in the pig pen but whatever it was it worked.

At that point I know I was not any kind of angel, I started doing drugs and drinking. It was not long after that I made getting high to escape reality a daily event. I know now how to party, and I had my reasons to party all the time.

I worked construction full time as a framer carpenter. I actually started construction when I was much younger. I worked for my Grandfather setting forms and tying steel. The first day for a hammer then a tape measure until I had all my tools.

To leave school I had to go through an independent living program. A 90-day program that only took me 6 months to do. I was then considered an adult with none of the privileges and all the consequences.

It was called by most the Lame Ass Project or Blame Us Project. It was across from Freedom Park. That was when I met Willard the rat. He showed me how to sneak out the window, how to get bear and get drunk in the park. He was my best friend until his premature death a few years later. He got drunk and rolled his car. He bought a Malibu just like mine and ended up dying in it. I also had another friend in there Johnny Rotten.

We would all smoke weed after our group meetings and escape reality. Once I was awoken in the middle of the night by someone shaking me. But when I woke up nobody was there. The house was in flames and I had to wake everyone up. All together there were 11 of us living there. We all got out ok. Again, and again I keep escaping death.

I worked hard and I played hard. At sixteen I had a place with a roommate who was 25. Tim worked with me and soon became like a real brother to me. We had several parties and there was always the drama with the girls.

I had one girl try to get me into a fight one time in my own house. I had no worries with my two best friends then, Derek and Romon we really knew how to party like the professionals, and they were like my regulators.

Once while playing catch with the Boneman, Romon, somehow accidently the ball fell in the porta potty and it turned blue. Thankfully, it had just arrived for the party and had not yet been used.

I say, "Hey Bonehead go long dude!" showing off because he is the most athletic of our crew, he starts running. Throwing a soaking wet nerf football dripping in blue stuff, was like throwing a wet sponge and it blew up on his chest when he caught it. I remember him just like I heard him yell so many times before scream at me "You bastard!"

Old Bonehead was so fun and so fun to pick on. Big kid with short black hair. He said he was Italian. He could sing and play guitar impressively. He liked to play with fire dancing and all the girls loved him.

We had tons of fun partying and stuff, I believe mostly to escape the reality of constant police harassment it was extremely unfortunate for me that I could not just go to my parents and tell them what was happening to me or how I felt about cops.

My Dad had been deputized into the Sheriff's department to assist in the security at a local mall. He spent many years working with them and his acceptance to them meant a lot to him.

My Dad, or most people at that time for that matter could never believe that cops would ever have that kind of behavior. I was deemed a liar. That only worsened my decaying relationship with my father.

My Dad was a great man of integrity. Towards the end of his life he was a better man than ever. He was a great neighbor and friend to many. I remember him pulling over to help people he did not even know, to help them with their car problems.

He was always going the extra mile for everyone, only sometimes it seemed like we, his family, sometimes got left behind. At home behind closed doors I was afraid of him. He was always angry and had a mean look on his face. A very no-nonsense man and I was a total joker.

All my friends were afraid of him too and would never come over or would take off whenever they seen him. He never abused me though and he always worked himself to death for us.

At the end, a totally different man, not so ornery and very caring to us and to all who knew him. I am glad that I was able to somewhat repair our relationship before his sudden death. Officially they called it complications recovering from a fall. He was recovering in a rehab center and we thought he would be fine and coming home. Then he got pneumonia and died.

See you never know when your time is so do not procrastinate, Do the things you need to do before you die. It is too late to do it after we leave our physical bodies.

Just ask yourself if you just found out you only had a month to live, what would you do? I know when I thought I only had a very few minutes to live when a nurse put a mask on me for surgery. All I wanted to do was call my mom. So, I assume that would be most everyone else's priority too? I do not know. But make that list of important things to do and get them done so you do not regret it.

I did not have much of a relationship with one of my sister's or my brother. He used to beat me up all the time and tell me that I was adopted, that was until I was old enough to defend myself and then we just did not have anything else to do with each other anymore.

My oldest sister was always being swept off her feet by

guys. She had her own exciting life. She looked like a young bionic woman for a while. The guys would circle the block for just a glimpse of her and they would all compete for her attention. I do not remember seeing her a lot. She was such a beautiful girl; I am not sure what happened.

I am so happy to have had such a close relationship with my other sister Sharon. We were extremely close for all our lives until her premature death. She was just weeks from her sixtieth birthday when she was diagnosed with cancer. They gave her ten months to live and she did not live ten days. She was one of those first people who died from vaping. She smoked for many years and it was unproven popular science that vaping was safer than smoking. Anyway, she lost her voice and could not talk anymore.

She was the closest person to me and losing her took a major chunk out of my heart. I miss her but I know she is in a better place, better than this place for sure. Just before she died, she asked me if I would take care of her dog. I told her I would and soon after she was dead.

I know that dog was her most prized possession. He shadows me constantly even now as I peck out words on my keyboard, I have a tiny black chihuahua guarding me from evil. It's not his fault he is so small every time he sneezes he smacks his chin on the floor. Besides it is not the size of the dog in the fight but more important is the size of the fight in the dog.

We hung out and started partying at an early age. She would give me handfuls of weed all the time and we would be stoned most of the time.

At first, she had this Dodge Dart. It had a push button

transmission She totaled it when she was giving me a ride home from a friend's house. We were just cruising down the road and I guess she did not notice the light was red. I was not paying attention I just remember a car hitting us broadside. That Dart was struck by another car just behind my door crushing the back door right behind me.

The engine started screaming and accelerating as we spin around in a complete circle in the intersection and then straight into Mannie's bar and grill. I say Hey Sis you just turned Mannie's into a drive through. the car was inside the bar and we stopped next to a table just before hitting the bar tender.

I remember someone asking if I were ok or if they could help me, so I ordered a garlic burger and a bud. I was underage and I think that was the first time I seen a topless dancer. Thanks for that memory Sis. She was ok and I was ok, but it was another close call.

We went everywhere together. For a few years that she did not have a car, she rode on the back of my motorcycle. Even in the wintertime we would drive my bike through the snow, and she would wipe the snow off my helmets face shield, with her gloves.

When she finally got a car, it was a 71 Datsun, P O S! It did, beat driving a bike in the snow but not by much. It would take ten minutes just to get up to fifteen miles an hour. Smoke would billow out of the back and it backfired all the time.

It also had a big rusty whole in the floor on the passenger side. I noticed it because sometimes if she drove through the water it would come up through the floor and get my feet wet. On rainy days I got used to picking my feet up a lot.

One time we were driving down the road and it was snowing, and the slushy roads were great for splashing blankets of mud, slush and snow on other cars and people as we plowed by. Share Bear, as I called her, had just dolled herself up so she could go meet this guy she had a crush on.

We are driving down this slushy road and the first puddle she hit sure enough came right through the floor and made a puddle. I look up, she just lit a cigarette and had a sneaky look on her face.

I turned to the road and seen this massive slush puddle coming up and she floors it. She thought that I was going to get soaked but I moved right out of the way of this tsunami of slush and mud just in time and she was instantly transformed into an ice sculpture.

She was frozen in time with the cigarette still stuck in her mouth, it was even frozen. I will never until my dying day and after I am sure I will never forget that moment. It is burned into my mind's movie forever.

BROKE BUSTED AND ALMOST BURIED

We got into trouble too. There was one time we were both in jail at the same time. I got busted for a drug possession charge. I had some weed and a pipe. I was going a bit overboard after divorcing my second wife. Drinking and drugs, girls, and parties all the time. I had this beautiful Victorian house, that is where I got shot later that year.

I am steadily declining in grace and stature. I started getting into trouble often and my mug shots could tell a story all on their own. The cops liked to do this, book, and release thing. They would not file new charges until you got out so they could put warrants out on you. This way they thought they could get added charges on people the second time they grabbed them. It worked too, people would go home get high and get a new possession charge.

I was partying so much that I knew that within a year I would be busted, broke, or buried. I did not know it would be all three. I was in jail because I had a half a million cash only bail (that is unconstitutional) and could not bail out. I was in there for 18 months trying to fight the charges. (so much for a speedy trial) Finally, they come to me and tell me "hey if you would have pleaded guilty you would be out by now. Plead guilty, your get time served and go home. I said I did not want to have it on my record. They promised if I plead guilty, I would get out and if I stayed out of trouble for seven years, I could get my record expunged.

I fell for their lies and plead guilty and the judge told me he did not have to give me time served, and he was not going to. I spent a few more months in jail before I could get out.

Then I got shot and stayed out of trouble for twenty years. Then when I tried to expunge my record. I found out that it, was bogus too. I tried to expunge it, but they said the judge cannot tell us what to do and because there were two charges instead of just one, they cannot do it. Nobody said I could not do it because there were two charges instead of one. They just said trust me and I would be ok. Load of bull! They got their conviction that is all they cared about.

I made the best out of my time in jail though. I went all the way from Minimum to super max and worked my way all the way back to minimum again. I even made trusty and worked in the kichen. I worked in the kitchen for a while as a trusty. The guards would always say, "What are you doing over here, I just seen you over there?" "I know I am just touring the jail." I'd say.

After preparing breakfast one time I seen the most horrible thing. We always had to mop and clean up and something said get out of the way! so I jumped back. Two inmates threw scolding hot water on two other inmates that were next to me and I see their skin slide of their muscles like melted cheese and butter. That was enough for me I decided I did not want to work anymore after that.

I think part of the punishment was the food. Lunch everyday was a bologna sandwiches with mustard and even if you do like that, which I most certainly did not, *every day?* Yuck!

Cereal for breakfast and the dinner menu did not change at all from week to week. Mystery meat, mystery meat stroganoff and mystery meat loaf. Friday we would have magic- must- go- mystery- meat leftovers. The magic part was surviving after eating it. You would barely survive, talk about cruel and unusual punishment.

Another weapon of torture was when we eat. Breakfast is at 6 am. Lunch is at 10 am and dinner would be at 2pm. Then you must go 16 hours before you can eat again.

The kitchen is only open for eight hours for overtime reasons. If you had commissary you could buy food and eat when you need to but if you do not, you will starve every day for sure. Oh, ya and you cannot save food and eat it later because then it would be contraband. Most everyone I knew that went to jail, by the time they came out they lost so much weight they looked like they had been trapped in a fat farm for six months.

Then there was the sleep deprivation torture. They have bright lights on all day long and at night they dim them just a little bit but not enough. You cannot cover the lights and you cannot cover your face. Just when you start to go to sleep it is time to get up for breakfast.

Man, those guards are pricks. They do not just oversee us, they essentially enjoy, punishing us too. They would toss our cells throwing all our stuff all over the place. I found out that they also listen to your conversations.

They had speakers in the cells to make announcements, but I found out the hard way that they listen too. I drew a picture of Yoda from Star Wars and commented "hey this looks kind of like Officer Taylor don't it?" I got a few laughs and then we went into total lockdown. Taylor came straight to my cell and ripped up the picture.

On my jail tour I learned how to hot wire cars, open locks, and all kind of interesting things. Even money laundering was easy if you know how. I got my PHD in street pharmaceutical productions and street pharmacy sales. The world could have been at my fingertips when I got out if I wanted. It was like college for criminals.

Because of my feelings towards the police I gravitated towards the "stoner" type of crowd. I remember experimenting with weed for the first time and how at first, I would have uncontrollable laughing fits with hilarious and delirious moments followed by intense deep thoughts and conversations.

It was when I was stoned, I would come up with my greatest ideas and when the high subsided for the most part my great ideas would subside as well. I like having my hair grow long. I have blond hair with blue eyes and looked like I could have been one of the guys like Sean Penn, that fell out of the van on Fast Times at Ridgemont High.

I missed out a lot not finishing high school and getting a job. I was though, immensely popular with many kids my age because I had my own place.

Nobody else my age had their own place. I was always at the party because the party was always at my house. I never had to pay for anything, and I was always happy.

That was the Anna Era in my life. Ridiculously cute

strawberry blond with the most beautiful eyes. My first real girlfriend. Why was I so stupid that I finally lose my cherry and now I go sex crazy and cannot get enough action. I guess it is just hormones, but I was out of control and could not help it for some reason. She was the sweetest of them all, but I was young, dumb, and full of bull.

Kelly was my first puppy love; Anna was my first intimate girlfriend. Julie was an outrageously cute blond-haired blue-eyed valley girl and first fiancé, and Lonna, she was my first wife. There was nothing wrong with any of them.

They were all great beautiful, smart young women but for some reason it just would not work out. It was a cycle that kept repeating itself only as time went on each relationship would be somehow worse than the last one was.

THE HAZY YEARS

Smoking weed was a great escape from reality. At the age of 14 I was just getting into Pink Floyd's The Wall, and Rush's 2112. I also loved Ozzy Osbourne's Crazy Train and Kiss's Love Gun. I loved everything from Firehouse to Boston, REO and Styx. I loved heavy metal and all those 80's hair bands.

There will never be anything that will ever match all that awesome heavy metal music we heard growing up then. It was so cool getting high and spacing out on that music, it seemed like time sailed on by. I also loved going to rock concerts.

My first concert was The Commodores and the next night I went to Kansas Audio Visions and there was no comparison, Kansas kicked ass and I never went to another disco event again. Lionel Richie would end up being fantastic on his own for many years. Where is Kansas now? My brother was a year older than myself; he was the one who was the "Disco Duck."

He was a straight A student and made himself somewhat successful in his pathway of life. I believe that was because he was given that chance, a fair chance, which was something I was not given.

Getting wasted and going to concerts was awesome. That Kansas concert was so cool but some chick sitting behind me, my sister, and her husband, drank way too much and barfed all over my sister's husband Ralph. Karma came into play because Ralph later he turned into some kind of a "barf" himself. It was then that I discovered rock rules!

In school, well when I was in school, there were all the cliques. The jocks, the preps, the teacher's pets, or straight A students, the nerds, and yes, the stoners, like me. I seemed to get along pretty much with everyone then, probably because I was the class clown and loved to joke around so much. I absolutely thought that was more important than my studies.

In class one time someone said, "Shut up!" or something like that, and the teacher said "Hey, in my class room there are three things I do not ever want to hear you say; number one, I don't care, number two, stupid, and number three, shut up." I yelled out "Shut up stupid, I don't care!" The entire class roared out in laughter and from that point on I took on the obligation and responsibility of being the class clown. The teacher did not find that so amusing.

It is disheartening but my own fault that when people ask me if I had a favorite teacher, I cannot think of any. I hated school and school did not like me either. It did not take too long to get a bad reputation. I started smoking cigarettes on top of everything else.

Once on the first day back to school from summer vacation I got caught smoking by the principal and was suspended. The first day back, and I think I set record. I retaliated and filled his car up with snow. I was not always a terrible kid but at that point my childhood was stolen, and my innocence was lost.

My best friend at the time had a Yamaha YZ80 and got

me into riding motorcycles. When I got my first bike it was on, we were out of control jumping, racing, and terrorizing our neighborhood. We used to do some way crazy stuff back then. I am sure my guardian angel had her hands full with me that time.

We went to see one of the greatest movies made back then, "Tommy;" we must have seen that movie 20 times. It was a rock n roll musical I still remember the music like it was yesterday. "The Who," another killer band. "See Me, hear me, touch me, feel me," were the words to another deep song.

I hope you know the one I am thinking of and it gets stuck in your head for a minute.

Going to concerts and movies like Tommy, and going to parties, was the best memories in this life at that time and yes smoking a lot of pot. I smoked so much pot I think I was pretty much stoned for three decades, but it did not take that long to graduate to other forms of drugs and alcohol.

Drinking, well I was way out of control drinking for a while. You know you are drinking way too much when you cannot say "Thanks for being hospitable," and people think you are trying to say, "Take me to the hospital." I am surprised I have any memories or brain cells left at all. Numb from everything good and bad. Stronger and stronger I felt an emptiness growing inside of me and I could not fill it with anything.

I was a member of the crowd that had long hair and liked to party and that was the kind of person the police loved to focus on. I liked having long hair, but I hated all the stigma that came with it. You know what I mean if you ever have long hair, people judge you like you are not honest or something.

I was driving down the road one time and I see this old guy probably ninety years old laying in the street next to his bicycle. I pull over and run over to help him up. Another lady made her way to him just about the same time. We helped him stand up and while she was steadying him, I reached down to pick his bike up for him, and he thought I was trying to steal it! Come on man I was trying to help you out. Nice, how everyone judges you.

Back then it was ok for cops to randomly pull you over and search you, and if you had long hair you were a prime target. I was already a prime target in Sunset City anyway, so I did not find any reason to hide my feelings towards any cops.

I loved girls too, like that old saying drugs, sex, and rock and roll, it was what I lived for. I think if there were anything, I regret it would be that I was a total ass to the girls I went out with. I loved girls but I could not have just one I had to have as many as I could, and I am sorry for all the hearts I broke.

I wish I could turn back time just to change that one thing. I would like to make my pennants to all the girls I hurt and if you are one of them, I hope I get the chance to do just that.

If it makes anyone feel better, I spent several years wishing I had someone to think about when a love song came on the radio. I learned one of my greatest lessons, how it feels to have a broken heart. I had no idea that it was physical pain. I felt like someone stabbed me I the heart. I know I needed that, as much as it hurt and as lonely as I was, I deserved it.

What I did not deserve was the police harassment Over the years, I was harassed daily. It got to the point that whenever I seen a "pig" I would just run and hide to avoid harassment,

I even got into trouble for that once. I was hiding to avoid getting patted down and searched and I was caught by them again.

"You must have something to hide, why are you hiding?" I would not say anything. That time I had some CD's in my backpack, and they took them because they said I probably stole them. Every day my hatred for pigs grew more and more.

When I turned 16 and got my driver's license and a car, I thought I would be safe from them, but the harassment went to an entirely new level. My Dad helped me get my first car and I do not know if he knew what was under that hood or if he just did not care but that car was sweet. Betsy 1976 Malibu Classic with a 400 Rochester Quadra jet engine.

Oh, she was a genuinely nice car and it was beyond any doubt, she was fast. But no matter how fast your car is you cannot outrun a police radio. I did give it my best shot though a couple of times I got over 120 miles an hour. I only had my license for about 6 months before I had it taken away from me.

That car was the best car for picking up girls too. I do believe that chicks look at your car first and if they do not like it, they do not even look at the driver. It was baby blue with a dark blue half vinyl roof. I had big tires with keystone classic rims and this car was totally awesome.

I loved that car and wherever that car and I went it was fun times. We used to have this hill climb called The Widow Maker. People would extend their bikes out so they could climb up the side of this good-sized mountain. It usually turned into a three- or four-day party.

Crosby Stills and Nash would come and jam out every

year in Park City. That car had captain chairs in front so you could turn the seat around and close the door. You would still have plenty of room to crash out or make out. Betsy was so awesome, I know I had a lot of fun because I do not remember a whole lot.

ESCAPING DEATH

Now I was constantly being pulled over and my car would get impounded. By the time I turned 18 I had been to the detention center quite a few times all for "B S" reasons from smoking weed and underage drinking. By then I had dropped out of school, stopped going to church and started getting wasted every day.

I did not notice until later that no matter how much I drank or how many drugs I did, I did not ever overdose. I should have died so many times from alcohol poisoning or something, but I never did. It was like I was invincible.

I treated and self-medicated myself for depression with drugs and alcohol for many years. I would sit in my driveway and get as messed up as I possibly could before I would stumble into my room at night.

There were many times I amazed myself how I was always able to make it home without getting a DUI or something. I was surprised on how much my body could actually take. Like I said before, I should have died many times but somehow, I was invincible. I really was, and later in life I found, there was a reason why I did not die or stay dead.

I cannot believe how many times I escaped death. Looking back on it now it seems like it could not be true, but it is. I told you about the time I got my life saved by a bunny but it wasn't until I was recovering from getting shot that I truly started to think about how amazing it was and how many times and ways I escaped dying.

WORKING WITH THE BULL

One time when I was about 12, we were on one of our annual visits up to Idaho. That is where my Mom was from, my Grandfather had a dairy up there. My Grandpa was so cool! When I was five years old, he taught me how to lasso and I would practice on him. At that same time, he taught me how to sing "I'm Poppy the sailor man, I live in a garbage can, I love to go swimmin' with bear naked women and swim between their legs, because I'm Poppy the sailor man." I was five and my Mom did not like that song very much. He used to take me fishing when I came up to see him.

One time I was about the same age. I caught this little tiny 3-inch trout. My Grandpa said oh that is a pocket trout and he stuck it in my pants pocket. He gave it a little pat and said we can save that one for your mom. It flipped around for a minute then I forgot all about it. A couple days later when my Mom found it, I could hear her scream from down the street. Lucky for me I know when I need to stay away. He was so funny and probably where I got my sense of humor from. He died of emphysema. That was hard to see for me so young watching him slowly suffer and die. Saint Charles Idaho would never be the same.

We used to go up there every summer for a little while to

visit and help everyone out. One time, my Uncle and cousins were rounding up cattle and herding them all up to another pasture to graze. Most everyone had a horse to ride on, but I was just running along on the side.

We were trying to keep them all along one side of the road. The road we were on the speed limit was 55 and the cars would come flying past us. It did not matter that we had so many cows right there.

As we were herding them down the road, we came along a section of field that was fenced off with old logs and there was a bull in there. That bull seen us coming and I guess he was wanting in on some of those cows because he used his horns to literally tear apart that log fence, and he got out.

The bull started running along with the cows and we were all trying to keep them out of the road and away from the bull. Without thinking I ran right in between the cows and the bull, and the bull turned on me. Before my uncle could get there on his horse the bull charged right at me as fast as he could and right at the last second the bull stopped in his tracks. He looked right behind me then he darted back the other way.

I turned around to see just what it was behind me that spooked that bull back into the other direction, but I did not see anything. My uncle rode over there and was yelling at me that I could have gotten myself killed and I was lucky I did not get stomped to death.

It was not until later that someone said that there was another person on a horse behind me when that happened, but they did not see where the girl disappeared to after everything was said and done. We just figured she was in the right place at the right time and then went on her way.

One time I was driving tractors across the dry farm with my cousin Sativa, we had two different tractors. I would drive one and he would drive the other. You could get the RPMs up, spin the wheel, and each back wheel had its own break so we could spin out doing doughnuts and stuff.

Well one time we were doing that and at the same time I spun out going one direction he spun out going the different direction and we both hit each other. We crashed them both head on. Here we go again there is another close call.

They had a collie up there. It looked just like Lassie. That dog started barking and running down to the dairy. We think it is a wild predator of some kind and we grab our guns. We run across the street then through the pasture of cows. I can see the tall grass moving around in front of Sativa and he is ten feet in front of me. We come right up close to the dog he is growling and fighting with something, but we cannot see what. Just then I hear Sativa scream like I never heard him scream before.

His voice cracks out "SKUNK!" Before we knew it, it was too late, and he used his special weapon. We were covered, both of us with this gosh offal smelling spray. It was disgusting and repulsive. Our family could literally smell us coming home. He got it worse than me but, in his case, it improved his odor. We both had a similar smell for a while after that.

Lots of fun things you can do up here. We went skinny dipping one time and my aunt spied on us, the pervert.

When we were not getting sprayed by skunks or totaling

out the farm equipment, we used to go out shooting too. Well Sativa was more of a hunter than I was being the city boy.

We were driving up an old dirt road. We both had these tiny 22 Winchester rifles. I look way up the road and I see this crow land in the top of this tree. I had the rifle pointed at the tree, I put on the breaks and when I stopped rolling forward, I pulled the trigger.

Unbelievable shot the bird fell to the ground. I could not believe I actually hit it. I drove up to the tree and jumped down off the tractor to find that poor bird hopping around in a circle with half of its head blown away. Gosh you dumb ass! I yell at myself now I have to put it out of its misery and shoot it again. I never ever killed another animal again I felt so bad and I can still after all these years remember what that crow looked like after I finished it off.

HANGING IN THE
HAUNTED HOUSE

Another time I hung myself at a haunted house not to commit suicide but just for fun because I was frying on acid. My best friend Derick and I used to volunteer at a Haunted House for Halloween every year.

Maybe not as much for helping kids that needed help, but more because it was fun to dress up all scary and hang out with other kids our age. I did like the fact although it was for a noble cause and even back then I did care about helping kids a little bit.

Maybe because of what a crappy life I had growing up. I hope that I can make some kind of difference for anyone, even if it is not huge.

Anyway, we were all dressed up and walking around scaring people and there was a dummy hanging by its neck and I don't know what made me think of it but I took the dummy down and put the noose around my neck and began pulling myself up into the air with my own strength.

I hung there for a few moments while Dereck laughed, and people walked by looking at me. I remember one person saying, "oh that is not real, its fake" and that was when I started slowly lowering myself down.

I did not let the rope slowly slide through my hands, I actually would let it slide fast for a few feet then grab on and stop and every time I did that, I would bounce a little bit with my entire body weight pulling on my neck. I do not know how I avoided breaking my neck, but I didn't. I did that three or four times until I finally hit the floor.

I looked up as some girl was looking at me and when I stood up and turned around to say something to her, she was gone. I do not know for a fact that hanging myself like that would have killed me, but I think it could have.

I could have put myself into a wheelchair for the rest of my life. I do not know if it was the acid but for some reason, I thought it would have caused much more pain than it essentially did. I really did not give it much thought after that, although I did have a nice rug burn for a while on my neck. Small price to pay for escaping death.

INVINCIBLE OR
JUST LUCKY

One time I was almost shot by the cops. At that time, I had a Subaru Brat and worked at Solitude Ski Resort as a lift operator. I was working repairing one of the lift chairs grinding a weld and I got some metal shards in my eye.

I was able to drive myself to the closest hospital and I was in there for several hours. I do not know how things are where you live, but here if you go to the emergency room count on being there for a while.

Anyway, after I left there, I started driving down the road and here we go again I am getting pulled over. I pulled over and before I knew it, I was surrounded by several cop cars. They all jump out of their cars and surround me with their guns drawn and pointed. Yes, both my favorite "pigs" were there, and I knew that they would have loved to be able to shoot me and get away with it.

One of them in front of me yelling "Hands up!" and the other at my side pointing his gun at me yelling at me "Turn off your truck!"

I am surprised that they just did not start shooting. Every time one would yell for me to turn off my truck, and I would reach down to turn off my truck, the other one would scream at me to keep my hands up. No matter what I would do I was going to get shot. Back and forth one would yell one thing and the other would yell something else.

I would try to comply to one and the other would yell something else. It was like they had it all figured out no matter what I would do they could shoot me for not doing what they said.

They would scream at me try to get me to lower my hands to turn off my truck and then shoot, I think the only thing I had going for me was a lady sitting on her front porch watching the whole thing. The entire time after attempting to turn off my truck, just when I thought they were going to shoot, the engine just dies.

Then they had me put my hands out the driver's window and they ran over and pulled me out of the truck through the window and threw me on the ground. They cuffed me and one of them pressed his knee into the center of my back.

I was thrown into the back of the cop car for about 45 minutes. I asked them what the hell is going on and they told me that I fit the description of someone who just robbed the bank. I told them I was in the hospital for over three hours and had the release papers on the seat of my truck to prove it.

That saved my butt and they had to let me go which they did but not without dragging it out for as long as the possible. To top it all off they gave me a ticket for improper lane change, I guess I forgot to signal for a full three seconds before changing lanes when they were pulling me over.

There were so many times that I could have died but there was a reason why I lived. I could go on describing almost endlessly all the times I escaped death. Like one time, for example I was almost kidnapped and beheaded in the Philippines.

I will go into more of that, later because it is such an amazing story. So many amazing stories, I know now all this time I was not invincible or just lucky I have had a guardian angel.

MY GUARDIAN ANGEL

It seemed like in every instance I escaped death, I seen a familiar face. It was my Guardian Angel, there helping me every time. I did not even notice until later when I thought about it.

She was there when I was driving too fast and she made me slow down. She was the candy striper. I ran out in front of a charging bull, but he turned and ran the other direction and she was there then too. I did not know who she was, but she was there. I believe that she was the woman sitting on the porch when police were shouting and pointing their guns at me. There were so many other times she guided my life until I finally figured out what is really important in my life. I know she is still here, and I know that I have made her job a little bit easier now that I am making better decisions.

I know we all have spirit guides who are there to help us. Most of the time they are distant relatives or loved ones who have passed over. Sometimes they are our soulmates from a past life, but I know we all have spirit guides. They help us with our lives by influencing us to do what is right because they care about us. They deliver our messages for us; they also hear our prayers, so they know what we want and where our heart is. They help us, guide us, and love us.

STRUGGLING BETWEEN GOOD AND EVIL

I used to go to church, but I stopped that at a young age. When I started doing drugs I dropped out of school and I really did not care about anything but getting wasted all the time. I did that for many, many years up until the time I was shot in a home invasion. It was in 2001 about a month after 9/11. It was when I was 37 years old. My death day, October 8th, 2001,

From about the time I stopped going to church until I got shot, life was basically all about getting wasted. Wasted is really a correct way to describe it, it was for sure not productive. We worked hard but we played hard too; skiing is a one of our favorite things.

Bonehead and I were in Honeycomb Canyon skiing the trees for fresh powder. We had a routine where we would always go. One time I was in front of him and decided to try a new direction. I am hauling down the powdery grove of trees and slowed down a second to stop.

The next thing I know I am falling straight down. It was about a fifteen-foot drop right into a pile of soft snow. I landed right on my butt. I hear Romon yell "Hey, how is it over there?" I yell back "It's awesome dude follow my tracks and go as fast as you can!"

"Here I come!" he yells back. Twenty seconds later I hear him coming and there he is flying right over the top of me.

"YOU BASTARD!" The only other time I actually, did, piss my pants laughing. He landed perfect though and kept on going. He really was good at everything he did.

The last time I played a joke on him though, it did not turn out so funny. All three of us were driving to dude's house to score on some chronic. "Hey Bonehead, you can't go in with us so hop out," I said. "Just start walking down this road and we'll pick you up in 15 minutes." He agreed and hopped out. On the way back we see Bonehead and I tell Derek "Hey check this out." I swear I didn't plan it this way but by the time we caught up to him he was walking across a bridge.

He does not turn around when we pull up behind him and I lock up the breaks. They screech out loud and I blew my horn. That stupid bonehead jumps over the guardrail of the bridge, scared he was going to get hit by a car.

Derek and I freak out because we know it is over thirty feet onto train tracks and there was a train rumbling by. We jump out of the car and run to look over the edge and he is hanging on to a patch of weeds and grass.

Thank God we were able to pull him back over again. I am like "Dude what the heck, why did you jump?" He replies you know "You really are a bastard, you know?" I felt so bad I gave him a free shot, but he did not take it. That was the last time I did something stupid like that to him.

As my addictions spiral out of control the emptiness

grows deeper and deeper. What goes up must come down, a rollercoaster of emotions increases day by day.

I loved to party. Although from the beginning of that period I started feeling that emptiness just growing inside of me. I could not get rid of it or fill it with anything, and I tried just about everything. I could not fill it with dope or alcohol or girls. No matter what, that emptiness would not go away; it just kept getting bigger and deeper with every passing day and with every passing day I was struggling between good and evil. I was my only and favorite victim.

The one thing I did do was work hard and kept a job. I had to support my habits somehow. I was a painter and I was good at that.

I liked painting big jobs like schools and hospitals, but I could do any project that came along. I would work hard all day and party every night. Through most of my difficulties my Mother was there for me. She always tries to be so witty and funny. Sometimes a bit off with the timing but she tries.

She is really funny when she is not trying. One time sitting at her kitchen table she was munching on chocolate orange sticks. I sit down next to her and I have a doggie treat in my hand. They are both about the same size, shape and color and she was not paying the best of attention to what she was doing. She reaches over and grabs the doggie treat and pops it into her mouth. She then hurries and spits it back into her hand and tries to replace it without me noticing. I laughed so hard I could hardly ask her how her doggie treat tasted.

Another time when she was concerned about her weight she heard that if you find a picture of a morbidly obese person and tape it to the refrigerator then that would give you motivation to stay away from the fridge. Well she could not find a picture of a morbidly obese person, but she did find a picture of a really gorgeous girl in a bikini swimsuit and put it on the inside of her fridge for motivation instead. Well this had adverse results, she did lose about 10 pounds, but my Dad gained about 40.

MYSTERIOUS AND
BEAUTIFUL

One of those nights partying, I was shot in a robbery. I call that my death day. I was seeing a young woman at the time named Hillery, but we all called her Hills. It was a year or so later that I found out that it was Hills who was behind the whole robbery thing. It was her idea and she was the one who invited the guys over who shot me. I was not well off by any means, but I guess I did have things that she wanted for herself.

It was almost a month after 9/11, October 8th, 2001. I spent the last few months on an almost constant party after my divorce from my second wife. I had spent quite a few years as a hardworking and dependable painter who, rarely took vacations and worked more weekends than I took off. I figured it was time I spent some time enjoying my life for a while. I thought the party scene was the way to go; I was my only and favorite victim.

Mysterious and beautiful enough to let your guard down. Another one of my vices was and still is to some extent, women. I have a weakness for women because women can be so beautiful.

God did an incredibly excellent job when he created women, in fact that was probably his greatest work. I have been married for over twenty-five years now but whenever I tell anyone, I must admit that all those years were not with the same woman.

I have had six serious relationships in my life up until now. I do not have a problem with commitment now but unfortunately that was not always true. One of my biggest mistakes I ever made was not being faithful to my first wife, but I know that if you learn from your mistakes, then they are lessons.

That was one of the hardest lessons I ever learned but since I did learn that lesson, I never cheated on any girl again who I have made a commitment to.

If you do not believe me you can ask my ex-wife, my next wife, my wife, or my girlfriend. That was a joke! I do not have a next wife.

I love to joke a lot in fact some will say too much but I think it is fun to always try to be happy. It was not always that way in fact I do believe that I have had many moments of my life when I was sad and lonely. I believe that was because of the bad karma I created for myself because of how I hurt all the sweet girls that I knew.

It is so important I know now that you try to treat everyone as kind and caring as you can. I know that is not easy to do, especially if you like to joke all the time.

I remember one time I was working and a fellow employee said he likes to splash chilly water on his face every morning to help keep him looking young and I told him "well now we all know that doesn't work." Although that did get some laughs it did hurt his little feelings and he was mad at me for a long time.

Some people just cannot take a joke. Be careful what you say because the smallest things can make the biggest impact and end up biting you in the butt. Now days you cannot even give a compliment in the office without getting into trouble for sexual harassment. No joke I told a girl she had a nice smile and was reprimanded.

It is easy to make fun of people sometimes, but it is not worth it. I would try to caution you to not make that mistake, so you do not have to learn that lesson the hard way like I did. Unfortunately, I did have to learn many lessons the hard way and a lot of times it did limit the number of friends I had.

I never did completely figure out women, I thought about it and thought about it and the only thing I figured out was thinking about it makes my head hurt. I do know that they can be as mysterious as they are beautiful.

MY DEATH DAY

I had just bought a Victorian style home and it was a great party place for me and a growing number of friends. Approaching 2:30 A.M. on my death day partying was coming into full swing. Two young men whom I had never met came to the house as guests of Hills; it was the perfect set up for a home invasion.

A loud knock at the door interrupted my friends and I. Hills escorted me as I went to the door. I invited them to come in "I hope you don't mind" said Hills. I let them in; we walked into my bedroom and picked up the partying where we had left off.

Not long after that, one of them pulled out a gun, it was a 38. He then started yelling at me "Give me your money, give me everything!" He was pointing the gun mainly at my chest but also at my other guests.

I did not even think about it a single moment, I just acted. If I would have thought about it, I am sure I would not have done what I did next.

I do not know if it was bravery or a stupidity, but my impulse was to act and not think, so I did. I just acted like Jacky Chan or Bruce Lee and did what they would have done in the movies or tried to anyway. Let us just say it worked out better in the movies. I took a swing at the gun. When I hit the barrel of the gun with my right hand it turned in the shooter's hand and pointed at my right side. That was when the first bullet exploded from the nozzle and went in and then out my right side.

It traveled through my body and then into the desk behind me, just inches from Hills, their accomplice.

The first shooter kept turning and then the second bullet hit me in the chest and that is where it still rests today. I found out later that they leave bullets in people all the time. One doctor told me that bullets are only dangerous when they are moving. I thought I was protecting Hills, but she was probably the safest one in the room at the time and stood to make out with most of my money.

My adrenaline was pumping out of control, probably from a combination of the excitement and the glass pipe we were sharing.

The gun hit the floor and I started punching the shooter in the face. He turned and started running towards the back. I chased him through the house and caught up with him five feet from the back door. Again, I started punching him and he hit the floor covering his face.

At this point his partner rushed in and I could not see him standing behind me. He also had a gun, it was a 22 pistol; he shot me two times in the back, point blank. Those two bullets took the fight out of me, the party was officially over at that point. Later I found out that those bullets took out my heart, lung, bowel, bladder, my small intestine, and my esophagus.

I hit the floor and called out to my roommate Larry, an exceptionally large ex-M.P. from the Marine Corp. When the two shooters heard me call for him, they hit the bricks as soon as they could. It sure is amazing how gunfire can clear out a room?

Larry rushed into the room along with Hills, I was lying on my back. I felt my right lung filling up with blood, so I turned onto my left side. Hills was holding up my head and crying, "Please don't die!" Not long after that but before the Police showed up Hills vanished.

The police started asking me questions, "Who did this?" I was trying to keep myself from going into shock. I should have said "Ask Hills, they were her friends," but she apparently bailed when she seen the police. Instead I just said, "Get me an ambulance."

The ambulance soon arrived, and the paramedics started working on me right away. They told me they were going to roll me over on to my back, but I told them "I can't lay that way because my lung will start filling up with blood."

MY RIDE TO THE HOSPITAL

They rolled in a gurney, put me on a back board keeping me on my left side and then strapped me on the gurney. As I was loaded into the ambulance, I kept my cool talking to them all the way to the hospital. I knew from experience that you can keep yourself from going into shock and that was the best way to survive any traumatic injuries.

I noticed that in the emergency lane of the hospital, the doctors and nurses were waiting outside for my arrival. As soon as the gurney hit the ground, they started working on me. First a nurse started cutting off all my clothing and I remember thinking to myself how cute she looked in her uniform and then told her that I generally don't go this far on the first date, but I would make an exception in her case. She had an unusual look on her face, and I wondered just what she was thinking.

She then put a mask over my face; I put my hand up to stop her and said, "no don't put me to sleep, just fix me while I am awake." She said "no, you're going to sleep but don't worry you'll be ok we are the best around." She put the mask on me, and my thoughts soon were on my family, and my mom, I did not think I had another fifteen minutes and I just wanted to tell my Mom "I love you" before I die. I spent the rest of my waking moments thinking about my loved ones. I did not want to go to sleep, I knew if I did, I was going to die, and I did die for a brief time.

Right after I remember a nurse putting an oxygen mask on my face I was weighted down with sadness. I thought of my family, mostly my mother. I thought about how much I loved her, but I did not have a last chance to tell her.

I was not afraid of dying I just felt so bad because I knew she would cry for me and I never wanted to make her cry. Everyone has a birthday and a death day only we usually do not celebrate the latter; well this was my death day.

MY NEAR-DEATH
EXPERIENCE

Suddenly I was not in pain anymore. I felt relaxed at first then I noticed myself in midair looking down at my own body, I knew it, I told her I didn't want to go to sleep, I knew if I did I was going to die! The tension was thick in the air. I could see the panic; I can tell that the people working on me were extremely stressed out. What is going on? It was then that I noticed the light, a light that was getting brighter and brighter.

It was brighter than the noonday sun and still it increased even brighter moment by moment. It was changing, I was changing. This transformation was incredible no words can explain how magnificent it felt.

Then I remember seeing like a sun shadow. It was like a shadow you would see on the ground when walking on a bright sunny day only exactly the opposite. It was light, it was a light within a light with light radiating from it; bright, almost blindingly. I could hardly look at it, but it was way off in the distance like at the end of a long tunnel.

Then I remember my substance, pure energy. Not solid but more electric type of matter. All my physical being is gone but

I still know I am a separate being with acquired knowledge. I have a personal identity. I have had Earthly concerns taken off from me and a sense of peace taking over my being.

White billowing clouds began to fill the room and surround me. I felt weightless as I began to rise higher up into the air. The clouds opened around me and welcomed me in like a warm blanket.

I was surrounded by gold chains hanging down suspended into the unknown and holding crystal stairs. I was gliding up the stairs gracefully only making contact with every other three or four.

I raised my head up to see beams of light reaching down around me. I felt my being completely filling with energy, almost an electric like sensation. It was almost like being under clear water how the rays of sunlight surrounded me and rose above my head into the air unsure where they went to or how far they go.

The energy was still increasing in my body getting stronger and stronger until I felt like I was about to explode only not painfully, it was exhilarating, it was fantastic, it was wonderful I wanted to burst.

I remember arriving to a place of extreme beauty; I do not think it was heaven I believe it was the spirit world. Fields of flowers, colors that I never have seen before, they were so beautiful. I was a painter and I thought I knew every color possible, but I was surprised at the combinations of colors, shades, and vibrancy.

The sunset and the clouds and the sky were also so beautiful more than I had ever imagined, in a way similar to Earth but

I knew this was not Earth at all. There was beauty all around but not like I had ever experienced before.

I remember looking at myself I was younger and somehow renewed. I looked at my body and where I had scars, I had no scars anymore and my only tattoo was gone as well. I had to be resembling my best state of health of my physical life. I felt great, no pain or anything bad. It was remarkably exhilarating!

I was drawn through the fields to a place covered by mist, and fog like clouds to a small group of people my own age, like myself. They turned and looked at me and they welcomed me with open arms. I did not recognize them but somehow, they seemed so familiar.

REMEMBERING MY
GUARDIAN ANGEL

I remember one face and that face; I knew I had seen her before many times before. I know I have seen her every time I had a near death experience.

She was there when I almost hit that rabbit. She was there when I hung myself. She was there when I was in that car accident. She was the girl behind me when I faced down that bull. She was there when I saved a girl from drowning. I do not know who she is, but I know she must be my guardian angel. She must be my spirit guide.

I know her from somewhere else, I just cannot put my finger on it. I reached out for her, but I was stopped in my tracks. I wanted to continue on, but I could not. I could not go any further; I was denied any further advancement. But why? Why couldn't I go on? I did not know why; all I knew was I wanted to, but I could not.

It was unbelievably sad. A feeling of sorrow came over me like I had never felt before in my life. Why couldn't I go on? It was like someone showing you something wonderful and then not letting you have it; it was not fair.

My last look at her warm eyes seemed to put me generally

at ease, in a look she told me it is not my time yet. And then I remembered her. We were together in a past life. She is my soulmate. No wonder why I could never have a relationship work out. It is because I truly did have a successful relationship, it was with her.

Scenes of us together in this past life are now in my mind. She was like a teacher or a nurse working with little kids. I was a simple farmer and we lived in a state of poverty.

The town looked like it had been built up and broken down several times. There were signs of battles taking place. People did not seem to have any care about humanity. But she was a sight for sore eyes. She was the most beautiful woman I had ever seen, and I knew we had been together in a different lifetime. I felt full and not empty anymore. My love I have finally found you. Now I must go, it is not fair!

So, we were together in this other life and when that life was over, I had to do it all over again, but she did not have to. I guess I am a slow learner or something. I know now that we come to this planet to learn things that we can only learn by getting a body. Once we learn that stuff, we do not need our body anymore.

So, this whole time she has been watching over me helping me, protecting me, and influencing me to do what I need to do so we can be back together again. As I remember it that was my near-death experience.

LIFE GOES ON

The next thing I remember was feeling pain, extreme and intense pain. It was eleven days later from the time the nurse put the oxygen mask on me. I had endured four major surgeries to save my life. My survival amazed everyone, I should not have survived but I did survive, why I did, now, I finally know why I survived. What I have left to learn, I do not know that, and I have struggled over that for many years.

I knew there had to be a reason why but at that time it escaped me. Everyone I knew told me the same thing I should have died; I was lucky to have lived and there had to be a reason why I did live. Two bullets were taken out of me one bullet went in and all the way through me and I still carry one bullet in my chest.

I will never forget how intense the energy was that filled my body and how wonderful it felt during my near-death experience. I used to be afraid of dying but now I look forward to it. I do not have a death wish, but I cannot wait for the day to come that I can go back to the light. It will be a great and wonderful transformation.

DO NOT PROCRASTINATE

I was in a coma for 10 days and I remember my body was in immense pain for several weeks after I woke up. I also felt an intense body high from the electrifying experience my spirit had gone through. As time went by my electrifying body high slowly subsided and turned into a numbness that I still experience to this day.

Other things were made known to me from that experience, most important I know now that when this life on earth is over a new life begins.

You are relieved of all your worries and pain and problems and you begin an existence that is meant to be.

I know we must live our lives here on earth to learn what it is like to suffer, and to love, and to learn what pain is, and to learn compassion. We also have a chance to make choices and use our free agency to make decisions that take us down the pathway of our existence. That is what makes us who we are and who we will be.

When I was in the hospital most of my family could come and see me. Everyone except my one sister. I guess that the logic there was they thought that the shooters knew my sister and would follow her to my hospital room to finish the job. I was listed as John Doe, oh how creative. I am not sure who made that decision, she was the one sibling who I was the closest to. I am so glad I survived for her because it was so unfair that they would not let her in to see me, especially because everyone thought I was going to die.

I believe that just enraged her and she was so enraged it motivated her enough that she was the one who figured out who it was that shot me. I said it before, and it is my opinion that cops are not really that smart and where do detectives come from? Cops. So, my sister basically did their job for them.

She had them cornered more than once but by the time the cops finally showed up they were gone. Her persistence and patience did finally pay off and she was able to detain the shooters long enough for the cops to get there and arrest them.

THE SHOOTERS

One of the shooters was an illegal alien from Mexico who had been deported several times. He was the leader of the gang recruited by Hills.

The other one was a seventeen-year-old kid who was a new member of this gang. The leader was a bad guy and I did not care if they locked him up and threw away the keys but the kid, I kind of felt sorry for him. I know that is stupid, I later found out that he lived with his grandparents because his mother was nowhere in sight and he never knew his father; I felt like he had lived kind of a hard life.

I know from my own life growing up that when you are young you make stupid decisions and mistakes, and I felt sorry for him.

Yes, he almost killed me, but I know that if he would not have shot me, they most likely would have shot him.

He was in the juvenile detention center, the same one I had spent so much time in, until he turned eighteen. On his birthday, they took him to prison, that is messed up. They were both convicted aggravated attempted homicide, that carried five to fifteen years. After five years I went to that kid's parole hearing to plead for his release.

He was surprised to see me there and even more surprised to hear me say "Give him a chance."

He wanted to change his life, I told them to "Keep him on a short leash and if he messes up then bring him back, but just give him a chance."

I know he said he wanted to get out and go back to school but I do not think they gave him that chance, because I would think that they would have told me if they did. I never heard if he ever got out and it has been over fifteen years.

I hope he did, and I hope that he is making a happy life for himself.

I know this sounds so strange, but it was easier for me to forgive him because I did not know him personally. I need to be able to forgive everyone and myself. I will keep trying and I hope that someday I can.

Another thing I learned is do not leave anything undone or unsaid because you never know when your last day will come. You never know if you are going to get shot or hit by a bus. That is why I always tell my mother I love her. Remember when I had that nurse put that mask on my face? I thought then it was too late.

Now I make sure that I never leave anything undone or unsaid.

You can choose to serve yourself or serve others like Jesus did, but it is your choice. I learned so much when I was having my near-death experience. I will do my best to share that with you because I believe that is one reason why I survived.

Like I said before even if we lived every day of our life here on Earth happy and never shed a single tear, we will still spend our entire lives suffering and in pain in comparison to what awaits us on the other side in our next life, in our next phase of existence.

I used to think that he who dies with the most toys wins. Now I know that is not what matters in this life. What matters is what you do with your life, did you make a difference? I hope I will because when I die, I know life still goes on.

When I woke up, I thought it was the next day, it was eleven days later; I had spent ten days in a coma. I had undergone four major surgeries; one being the most dangerous surgery known next to brain surgery, (emergency heart and lung surgery at the same time) I had two surgical teams working on me.

One team went through my chest and operated on my heart and the other team would go through my back to operate on my lung. There were so many stiches that they lost count after everything was said and done. The first thing I heard was something I never heard before in my life it was my Dad crying.

That cannot be, the most macho man alive and the one person who never showed a caring emotion, only grumpiness, crying. I honestly did not think he cared but I guess he did and just never showed it.

You're Outa Here!

After 21 days, I could pass a cardio and lung test and because I had no health insurance I was put into a wheelchair and literately poured onto the front lawn of the hospital. My hospital bill came to eight hundred and seventy-nine thousand dollars. Can you imagine almost a million dollars, I would like to send that bill to Hills just to see the look on her face.

I had lost everything I owned. At the advice from the doctors my parents prepared me for my funeral. They sold all my stuff and bought me a nice burial plot, but to everyone's surprise I did not die, or I did not stay dead.

I do remember having some memories of being out of my body and looking down on different scenes a couple separate times, once in the operating room and once in the recovery room. I knew I should have died or should have stayed dead that time.

I know now how I lived through it all, my guardian angel. I did not know why at that point, but I knew there had to be some reason why. I struggled for many years trying to figure that out.

I did finally find out so many reasons why I survived. The smallest of actions can affect generations.

One of the best things you can do for yourself, is not for yourself, it is for someone else. Every single one of us can make a difference. Let us all bond together and make a change. Long after the pebble has been thrown into the pond, its ripples continue to flow. Some may slow and eventually die but others may influence change to still waters and make permanent change to our surroundings.

It is our chance to make a difference what we do is who we are. Positive and negative change is at our feet, you cannot stand idle and just hope things will work out. Either we are going to be successful or fail and we cannot fail. Not only for the sake of our children who depend on us but for all children and humanity.

OUT OF BODY
EXPERIENCES

One of the things I remember from the spirit world is who I seen there; that was the last thing I remember before I came back. I have had a lot of out of body experiences since then.

It took me a long time to recover from heart surgery and because I lost my home and everything, my parents let me recover in their spare room. When I moved in there from the hospital, I thought I was having vivid dreams. I was flying through the air all over the place. I was going to places that I had never been to before in my life.

I was flying, not entirely effortlessly and I could not control where I was going.

When I had "out of body experiences", I would end up sometimes in the mountains and other times I would end up at the ocean but it seemed like many times I was going to places that I had never been to before.

I had dreams that I was in other people's houses whom I did not know, and they would either run from me screaming, or chase me around waving the Bible at me trying to get me to leave. I know it sounds crazy, but these "dreams" felt like I was a ghost invading other people's houses. I even went to entire villages and places where the entire town would chase me around and I could not get away. The only way I could get away was I would wake up and it would be over.

These were scary and violent dreams, at least I thought they were dreams and I even went to a doctor to talk about it and he tied it to PTSD (Post Traumatic Stress Disorder) from getting shot.

That just did not make sense to me. He tried to interpret my dreams by saying flying around in the air was my dreams telling me that I did not have any control of my life.

I even believed it for a while and thought that it may have even seemed to help me a little. At that point. I started seeing places that I went to in my dreams, places I had never been to in my conscious life. Now how in the world is that possible? As time went by, more and more times, I would recognize places that I knew I had never been to in my waking moments, but I knew that I had indeed been there.

I have seen places in other countries in detail that I knew I had never been to before, and then on top of that I seen a girl in the store who was in one of my dreams. I keep saying "dreams," but I know that I was not dreaming.

I was having out of body experiences when I went to sleep at night.

I observed this girl in the store, and when she first looked at me, she turned white as a sheet. It scared the day lights out of her, like she had just seen a ghost, like I was the ghost. She froze in her tracks, but I turned and walked away, and she did not say a single word.

I don't know if she put two and two together and figured out where she had seen me, but I remember seeing her at her house and I know I had never been there in my waking moments. I know she does live in my general area, but I don't know where and I have never been back to her house since I last seen her in the store and I have never seen her again after that.

I have never tried to go to any place specifically until much later. I would never intentionally scare anyone, and I would feel terrible if I did.

My Mother even told me that she woke up in the middle of the night and seen me or it was my spirit, standing at the foot of her bed. I scared her and then I left, and I went back to my body.

In the morning we both tried calling each other at the same time and it was then that my thoughts were confirmed. She told me she had seen me, and I told her I was sorry for scaring her. I knew then I was not just dreaming; I know I was having out of body experiences.

It took me years to try to control these events. Mediation is key for control, but I still have a long way to go.

AMONG THE LIVING

I know this sounds unbelievable and unfeasible; I know I would have a tough time believing it too if it had not happened to me.

I have out of body experiences about ten times a month now, but the more I am getting into meditation the more I gain control. Many things can be scary when we do not understand them, and this is definitely one of those things.

I do not think it is hurting me in any physical way but what about emotionally, it is possible. I thought about it and I believe that because I was in a coma for ten days, while I was under, I began to access a part of my brain that I did not regularly access before.

Now I am experiencing new memories and abilities that I did not have before. Or rather they were suppressed in my subconscious from past lives I have lived.

I have heard of cases when someone has suffered a head injury and now can play the piano. Another case a man experienced going through a coma, waking up and being able to speak French. I have heard stories that after head injuries many people report having all kinds of abilities that they did not have before.

I do not think that bumping your head is a magic way

to learning anything. What happened to these people and many other people, was the same thing that happened to me. We started accessing memories that were suppressed in our subconscious from our past lives.

I also think that people are in a way just like ghosts, and like people ghosts, can be good or evil. I know I am becoming more sensitive to new things. One thing I have become interested in and I have been trying to learn more about, is ghosts and spirits. One difference between the two is that unlike spirits, I believe that ghosts were at one time living people who had a body but never went to the spirit world after they transformed, and for that reason they didn't completely transform.

Some, probably many spirits, were never ghosts; but ghosts at one time were spirits before their physical life on Earth. For example, first we were simple spirits in the pre-existence. Then we are born and gain a physical body.

We live our lives creating karma and learning what we need to learn, to advance to our next phase of existence. This is where the difference comes in.

For whatever reason, some of us become attached to something or someone here on Earth, or maybe we are afraid to go to the light and meet our maker. That is when ghosts become earthbound, due to whatever reason they decided to stay here instead.

They are now ghosts, and they are incomplete since they did not go entirely through their transformation process. They were spirits, and then human, but now they are ghosts.

A ghost can cross over and complete its transformation

with help from a light worker, or when they have satisfied their attachment. Otherwise, a ghost can be trapped indefinitely.

Others did transform and are intelligent spirits because they did go to the light and did completely transform. A spirit has the ability to pass through different dimensions. Earthbound is one phase of existence. The Physical dimension is another, as well as the pre-existence. There are no limits to phases of existence.

They can be in their phase of existence and be able to go to lower phases of existence, coming to Earth to act as a spirit guide or a messenger. As spirits, we cannot advance to higher phases of existence until we learn how to move on to that phase of existence.

Our desires and actions determine what phase of existence we will go to next.

PASSING THROUGH DIMENSIONS

I believe that if you have children and they do not make it to your level or phase of existence for some reason, you can go to them. You can go to lower phases, but you cannot go to upper phases without learning how and earning the right to advance to upper phases of existence.

Being a ghost, you are basically trapped here on Earth in a dimension that few can see. There are people who know how to use a certain part of their brain; they are clairvoyant and can see ghosts and even communicate with them.

I believe that Heaven and Hell can pretty much be explained as different dimensions and states of mind where some people who have earned the ability can pass through, while others cannot. Earthbound spirits or ghosts may feel that the dimension they are in is a form of Hell or Heaven depending on their desires and actions.

There are also "light workers." Light workers are and can be anyone who has special abilities. Being able to communicate with those who have passed over is one kind of light worker. I am talking about messengers alive on Earth, spirit guides and guardian angels.

As I mentioned earlier, spirit guides are most likely a relative of yours who has passed away, someone who is attached to you, such as a soulmate from a past life, or someone you have cared for.

Everyone has at least one spirit guide or guardian angel. Angels are exalted spirits that help do God's bidding. I do believe that there are miracles performed everyday with the assistance of angels or spirit guides. Ghosts have their own reasons for why they are among us. Some spirits just want to stay among the living.

GHOSTS AND SPIRITS

I became interested in ghosts a few years ago when I had an interesting thing happen to me. When my daughter was a toddler, I wanted to build a room for her next to mine so she would be close to me.

After my minor remodel was completed, that was when strange things started happening to us. In the middle of the night I would hear noises coming from her room, and her toys seemed to be playing by themselves. I would investigate and notice her toys would be spread out across the room in an unusual way, other than the way they were left a few hours before.

I did not give it much thought until one night I was awoken by the sound of her monster bank roaring. It was just a toy, a little piggy bank that would roar when you put money in it, but it roared out loud unexpectedly in the middle of the night, so it startled me to say the least.

Well the other toys like the dolls and such I didn't care about or it really didn't seem to bother me much going off in the middle of the night, but the monster going off in the middle of the night, oh no way!

So, I grabbed it and took it straight into the garage where

I was sure that I would never hear it again and then I went back to bed.

I was laying there for a few minutes just about to fall asleep and I felt something touch my foot and out of the corner of my eye I seen a little boy just for a second standing there. I was startled but also felt bad that there was a little boy ghost in my home. However, that explained why the toys were being played with.

That night when I did finally fall asleep, I had a dream and I believe that it explained further why that child was there. He had died and was waiting for his mother to come and get him. When I woke up the next morning, I prayed in the name of Jesus to open the door to heaven and let him in; I told the boy that his mother was there waiting for him. I know I crossed him over successfully.

I felt happy that he was not stuck here any longer. I believe that it is so important to try to help everyone we can, even if they are no longer among the living.

Ghosts were people at one time, and I do believe that they too may need help whether they are ghosts or not.

There are also demons; demons are evil spirits that have never been given a physical body or born into this world.

DREAMS AND PAST
MEMORIES

Our brain is extraordinarily complex, and we will never unlock all the possibilities and abilities that we can accomplish with our brain, at least in this life. I have heard people explain that dreams are a way that the brain helps us deal with our everyday life, that makes some sense to me and I can believe that.

A good example would be that if you are stressed out about something in your life, like you are unable to catch up on your bills, you could have a dream that shows your life in a much worse state like being homeless.

Then when you wake up in the morning and you have a moment to think about that dream it will give you some relief about your present state in life.

This might make you feel that your life is not so bad after all. That would help you cope.

I know that not all dreams are just a figment of your imagination. I know that some dreams may be messages from the dead, like that little boy, while some may be designed to help you with your stress. Some dreams may be a flash back from the past or past life. I had a dream I was a fly, and someone was chasing me around trying to kill me. I now know for sure it was an out of body experience not a past life or crazy dream. There will be many times we will fail to understand our dreams.

I know that some of my dreams are small flashbacks of my past lives. I know that experiences I have had in my past lives have had some subtle influences in my present life. I believe that some of my fears I have now, originally began from deep seeded memories in my subconscious, in this life or others.

Fears and fetishes, likes and dislikes, influence us from the past. We accept our desires as just a personality trait in which makes us individuals. Nobody really questions why am I afraid of flying, or afraid of bugs? We just accept it and move on. There could be a good reason why you are afraid of flying because of an experience from a past life or other times that you once existed in. There are countless documented stories about people and children having past lives.

I believe that the experiences I lived through in other lives, has influenced my way of living and thinking in this life. I believe that I may have lived a hard life because of the karma I made for myself in the past. I also believe that is why I try so hard to help people who are homeless and hungry.

Those little flashbacks in my dreams and memories hidden in my subconscious from lives lived in the distant past often haunt me. This has an influence on how I am in this life; I believe that it has had an influence for good and for bad.

It may be why I have such a big desire to help others. It influences me to stand up in times of need and have courage when most people would run away. I may not be the toughest person, but I do have heart. I believe that our dreams can give us glimpses into our past.

Dreams are also a conduit for communication with loved ones who have passed.

I have had many dreams, some experiences I have not ever had in this life. I do know I have had these experiences, at some point, in one life or another, because they are reoccurring dreams. I also believe that déjà vu triggers memories like that as well. Do you know the difference between déjà vu and uva jed? Uva jed is the feeling that you have never been there before. I get that all the time!

NEW PHASES OF EXISTENCE

I want to point out that I know there are many parallels to what I learned in the spirit world and what people may learn going to church, but people who go to church may not always get it entirely right. I believe that there may be a little bit of truth in most churches.

There are some who are all so awfully close but are just not quite there yet from what I can see. I was not in the spirit world extremely long, but I learned a lot.

I know that when you are dead, time is of no relevance. When you think about it, the only moment when time is relevant, is when we are alive on Earth and we are aging, then we are getting older, so time matters. In our next phase of existence time may not matter.

Time is almost like a valuable commodity when we are alive on Earth; after we leave our mortal bodies, time does not matter anymore. Time is like a dimension that we cannot see, like how gravity is there but we cannot touch it. We will probably never fully understand it while we are alive on this Earth.

There is so much to learn. We will never understand everything while we are alive here, but we will eventually learn and understand all that we wish to know. In our next phase of existence and throughout all eternity we will always have the opportunity to learn and grow.

I used to have so many questions about God and religion before I got shot, things I never learned in church. But when I woke up from my coma, I had the answers to everything I had ever wondered about.

One of my questions was "How does God know everything you do? How does he know whether to send you to heaven or hell?"

The answer to that is, before we are born, while we are in our pre-existence to Earth, we were simple beings, spirits who did not understand much of anything.

There is so much that we need to learn like love and pain and sympathy, that we could never understand without getting a body.

We needed to get a body to learn so many things, so we came to Earth. When we are born, we have incredible organs such as a brain. It is inconceivable how marvelous this organ really is, we do not even use that much of it.

We only use a small part of our brain; if we could use our whole brain, we could make things levitate, we could communicate without talking, we would be telepathic. If we used all our brain, we could have extra sensory perception, we could be clairvoyant, and all kinds of things we could do if we could use all our entire brain right now.

There will be a time that we will be able to do all the things we want in the future if we so desire. If we make the right choices.

OUR LIVING MOVIE

When we are born, our brain starts recording everything we do from our first breath to our very last. We take our brain everywhere we go, and everything we do and experience and learn we save it all like our own little movie; all those memories are stored in our brain. Then we leave our body and have our magnificent transformation, we take all of our knowledge with us.

Have you ever heard anyone say when they have had a near death experience "I saw my whole life flash before my very eyes?"

When that happens, it is called total recall. When we die, we take all that accumulated knowledge with us. When we do eventually meet God, he knows everything we have ever done because it is right there with us, we have saved it, just like our own little movie and he can then see everything. I believe that we can learn how to watch other people's movie as well. In the future that will solve a lot of crimes.

RELIGIOUS PARALLELS

If there is something that you have done in your life that you are not proud of and you don't want God to see it, there is a way to erase it out of your memory. It is called repentance.

You must know that you did something wrong, and you must be sorry for it. You must make up for it like if you stole something from a store you have to pay for it. You must promise not to ever do it again and you must not ever do it again. You must ask for forgiveness, and you must forgive yourself. All these steps are vital.

It is so important to forgive yourself because if you do everything else and you do not forgive yourself it will stay with you in the back of your head in the form of guilt. It will not go away. If you can do all that it will go away, it will be erased out of your life's recording.

I learned that we advance from one phase of existence to another by gaining distinct levels of knowledge and experience. Knowledge plus experience equals wisdom. We must gain a certain amount of wisdom before we can advance to our next phase of existence. As I said before until we come to Earth and get a body, we do not know what pain and suffering is.

We do not know empathy or sympathy and many other things. We cannot learn many things without getting a body.

That is why we come here to get a body and learn so we can advance on to our next phase of existence.

When we die, we take all our acquired knowledge with us to the spirit world then there a decision must be made. Some questions are asked, did he or she learn what they needed to learn to advance to their next phase of existence? Can they keep learning what they need to here in the spirit world? Can they go back to their body if it is not too messed up and pick up where they left off, like I did? If their body is too messed up, can they then start over in a new body? That is called reincarnation. Resurrection is a revival of a physical body and reincarnation is reborn in a new body or host.

I know we can all have more than one life here on Earth in fact I believe that some people have had several lives on Earth. I believe that we even have a choice sometimes on what we want to do. We either move on to our next phase of existence or we stay in the spirit world to learn more there.

We could come back to keep learning here, which is what I did or if our body is too messed up to keep living. and we have not acquired the knowledge we needed on Earth yet, then we may get another chance in a new body, reincarnation.

I believe that we can also choose to reincarnate and have the choice to have as many lives if we want.

I learned that everyone goes through the same phases of existence, but everyone's phases of existence are different, they are unique to each person. We all need to acquire the same basic knowledge, but we will ultimately choose different pathways to get there.

The karma we create for ourselves will have the greatest

impact on our happiness. This is something I struggle with, sometimes even daily, but I am trying to get better.

I am sure we all have similar difficulties, some more than others. It is so important to be forgiving although it is not easy. There are members in my own family that make it so hard to be forgiving but I need to do it. It is also so important that we learn to forgive ourselves as well.

Nobody is perfect but we can all strive towards perfection so that we can all try to be the best that we can be. I wanted to share my experience with people who need to hear that after we die and leave our bodies it is not over; it is just the beginning of a new phase of existence.

WONDERFUL
TRANSFORMATION

There are a couple of reasons why I decided to author this book. One is I wanted to share some things I learned when I left my body and went to the spirit world. I was not gone long but I learned so much. It is hard to understand how I could have learned so much in such a short amount of time, but time is of no relevance when we are not trapped in the shell, of our human body.

I know how important it is to share what I learned for everyone who wants to learn answers about our existence. This is for clarity for those people who care to improve themselves, and the lives of those who they care about. I think that it was meant to be, for me to survive. I bring your message to life, that life as we know it is much more than we think. Living for an unknown amount of years, and then you die, and it is all over. When we die, it is not all over.

For many years science and religion have been in a kind of struggle against each other. For many people it is hard to understand what is true, science or religion, but really in many ways' science has backed up many religious views.

More than one mass cannot occupy the same space at

the same time and mass does not appear or disappear out of thin air, it evolves and changes. Like the burning of wood, it changes into smoke and ash, but it does not just disappear. In a way we transform like that but we as a mass transform into energy.

I know that as we grow, we take on mass and our bodies change. We had to take in sustenance for our bodies to grow. Some changes our subtle and some are more drastic and noticeable.

Some take many years, and some take truly little time at all. When I think about how some changes may be so drastic and hard to believe. I think about one fitting example it is how a caterpillar comes out of its cocoon for the first time as a new butterfly, what a wonderful transformation.

We may not make such a dramatic transformation during our lives but the transformation we make at the end of our lives here on Earth is much more dramatic than that of the butterflies. When our spirit leaves our bodies, it is the most wonderful transformation you could ever imagine, karma willing.

SCIENCE BACKS
UP RELIGION

I mentioned how science backs up religion and, in many ways, it does. The big bang theory is one explanation of how our universe was created. Those who believe in the Bible as I do, may believe that the Bible is true as far as it has been translated correctly.

I believe that the Earth is much older than the Bible suggests. That doesn't mean that some things in the Bible are or are not more accurate.

I do believe that over the years and as many times as it has been translated that there are things that have been mistranslated and even lost. Over the many years it has been available the Bible has been interpreted countless times. Although there are mistakes there are many things to be learned from the Bible.

I believe that the universe was created by a first-time major event that could have been just like science has explained, "The Big Bang." I do not believe that this event just happened on its own, something made it happen. There are powers beyond our comprehension that have control over everything as we know it and it was greater powers than we know that caused this first-time major event.

I have spoken to many people who refuse to believe anything that they cannot see for themselves, but I ask them are there sounds that they cannot hear? Sounds like the ones that only dogs can hear. Just because we cannot hear them, we know that those sounds are still there.

It is the same principle our visual spectrum is limited as well. We have good hearing and sight but just like there are sounds that we cannot hear there are also many things that are there that we cannot see.

We cannot see or hear everything that is around us. I know of a person who was taking pictures of deer in her back yard. She then posted them on social media. Almost at once she was bombarded by everyone who seen those pictures. The pictures revealed, believe it or not, flying saucers or UFOs. The pictures even made the local newspaper.

I also believe we should know that there is more than just dying and then going to heaven or hell. As long as we have the desire to learn and grow, we can advance from one phase of existence to the next. We have a lot of control on how far we go in the great scheme of things.

Many of us will get stuck in one phase of existence or another and will not be able to continue to advance. Some people will be satisfied and content in any specific phase, but others will grow and advance, learn more grow and advance further and further until they are content.

This process can continue repeatedly, over, and over again until, if we want to, we someday become what we understand to be like a God is yourself. As I mentioned before we can learn how to do things like levitating, communicating without talking and reading each other's thoughts and minds or even walking on water If we desire. Because we do not know how to do that now we think that only Gods can do that. Man has defined Gods to be of exceptional powers beyond comprehension.

WE GROW WITH THE UNIVERSE

We live in a vast universe that is continuing to grow as well. I know that if we advance and grow continually, we will eventually be able to create our own worlds just like this one. I believe in God, I also believe in fate, but I do not believe that I will ever be the same as or better than the all mighty God I worship.

I think that just thinking that would be wrong or blasphemy. I do believe that we all have the potential to be like what we believe Gods are.

Having vast knowledge and powers. We believe that only a God can do that because we do not understand how it is done. But we can learn how. Just because we do not understand now, does not make it impossible.

I know that much of this sounds repetitive, but we have a lot to learn. That is why we are here, to learn and to grow. Before we came here, we were simple beings that did not understand a whole lot.

The only way to understand emotions like the most important, LOVE. Is to get a body You could not ever know what pain is or to experience passion without getting a body.

I do not think there is any other way to learn those things and many other things, without a body.

There are many scriptures available that give us a little direction in our beliefs as to who we are and where we come from. The Bible is one I mentioned, it is basically a historical book about people and times that happened in the distant past.

There are many other books such as the Quran, and Torah, the Vedas, the To Te Ching, the Upanishads, the Bhagavad Gita, the Buddhist Sutras, the Book of Mormon, and many other ancient writings that are about people their beliefs, and their history on Earth.

These books also talk about God or beings with power and proclaim the way we should live our lives. The book of Mormon is the main staple of the Mormon religion, but it is a book that was written by Jews about Jewish families that existed many years ago, it was about how two families became great nations. I think that is an interesting fact about that book that most do not know.

Records from our past no matter where they come from if they are true, they can give us insight and direction for our future, which is why they are so important. In school we learn history to help us with our future. I believe that there are many things in these writings that are true and our given to us to help us in our lives. There are many examples good and bad in these writings that we can learn from.

These books are about a people who lived a long time ago. I believe that they all may have essential information for us to learn how to improve our lives. There are many examples from people who lived in the distant past.

TRYING TO UNDERSTAND

I believe that the Bible is awfully close to explaining to us many things, but I believe that we just do not quite understand everything in it exactly how it was meant for us. We are close but just do not quite understand everything. I am not really religious, but I am a spiritual person.

I am not saying that it is not important to become religious. I think that everyone should learn about religion and follow their beliefs. I do feel that for the most part, most religions help us to become better people and that is important.

It is even more important later in our lives when we have sins to be forgiven for to be baptized, but maybe not so much when we are young innocent children.

When I had my out of body experience there was many parallels to what I learned in the spirit world and what I have learned while going to church. The purpose of this book is not to try to convert people to religion, but to help people to understand that they have control over their existence.

I would be lying if I said I did not write this book for the money because I do hope to make some money from this book. It is what I want to do with the money I make from this book that is so important to me.

Not to make better life for myself, but my passion is

helping homeless children. Here and in the Philippines where children are literally starving to death. I have a Facebook page and if you have one as well you can go to the search window and type <u>Helping.homeless.children@Gmail.com</u> and my picture will come up and you can see pictures of the children who I am helping.

Be careful though because some of those pictures can be hard to look at. These children go to sleep every night with their stomachs hurting so bad because there is hardly ever any food in them.

Their organs are feeding on themselves and they are beginning to bloat which is one of the first symptom of dying of starvation. I cannot think of a worse way to die than to starve to death. I think I would rather be eaten alive by ants or sharks, at least then it would end quickly. They say that starving is the only way to die that it is impossible to die with dignity.

I hope to someday have a soup kitchen to feed these children. I want to give medical attention to them, and I want to educate them. I also want to start up an adoption program.

I want to build water purification centers. I want orchards and farms that I can produce food for all homeless and needy people here and all around the world. Yes, I have a lot of plans and high hopes for helping others and I hope this book can help me with that.

I tried raising money for many years, but people do not trust me, and I can say I do not blame them. It is too bad that so many people take money from people for charity and then spend the money on themselves. It is too bad people are so dishonest. It is also unfair that people who do this make it hard for those of us who are trying to do some good.

There is always a tragedy somewhere in the world that people are donating their money to.

Needless to say, it is not easy raising money. I have a Go Fund Me page to help homeless children and, in a few years, I raised 20 bucks, so yes, I hope that this book helps me with some of my high hopes.

PRAYERS CAN GET ANSWERED

I survived dying for more than one reason. I believe my daughter is one reason, she is my rescue baby, but I think she also rescued me as well. She undeniably helps keep me grounded. In part I dedicate this book to her.

About fifteen years ago I wanted a baby so bad and I know that it sounds funny hearing that from a full-grown man. How could I be baby hungry? but I was. I tried everything but no matter what I did, I could not get pregnant (joke) but I did spend one-night praying to God whole heartedly and saying that what I want so much in my life is to have a baby.

I was on a cruise at that time and the next day I came home, and I see my baby for the first time. I know for a fact that one, if I had not prayed for a baby I would not have met her and two, if I had not been in a position of helping people I would not have been in that position to have received my child. I know it was not just a coincidence as she was an answer to my prayers.

She was my gift from God I know that. I always tried to help those in need and at that time I had a construction company. One of my workers was homeless. He had a wife and baby which I helped off the streets.

I got them an apartment and he was working off the rent. When I got home from my cruise I went over to that apartment and that was the first time I seen her, her name was Uvia. I always thought that babies were not really that beautiful, but she was the prettiest baby I had ever seen.

I loved her from my first sight of her. She was beautiful just like the little Gerber baby. Her mother was homeless and needed help getting on her feet as well. She did not know me, but I think that something in her heart told her that I was going to be important to helping her and her baby.

I have had Uvia for the past fourteen years now and I hope that we have many more happy years together. I know prayers can be answered and I know dreams can come true.

Science has proven to some extent that the universe is billions of years old, if you can believe in science and I do. It is unfortunate that now days many people do not, or they choose to pretend that they do not.

There are now, there has been and there always will be many countless phases of existence. Phases of existence have been around since the beginning of time. As soon as time started, we had different dimensions and phases of existence. There were other dimensions and species here on Earth before we came to Earth. I believe that the Earth completely recycles itself every two to three hundred thousand years. It is estimated the Earth is three and a half billion years old.

Phases of existence can also mean different moments in time. Beings like ourselves and diverse kinds of beings have been passing through countless dimensions and phases of existences forever and this will be going on for eternity. I believe that I have had many past lives.

I know that we may not, and some of us cannot learn everything we need to learn in just one life here on Earth. Eternity is never ending there is plenty of time to learn what we need to learn because we will never run out of time Your physical life is temporary, but your spiritual life is eternal.

REPLENISH THE EARTH

On other planets, in the spirit world, and in other dimensions now and in the distant past, life has existed and evolved from the first big bang and will go on for infinity.

We as well as many other species have been living, learning, and growing for a long time; it will never end. When we leave our bodies and have this wonderful transformation into our next phase of existence. We will go to the spirit world and many things will then be made available for us to understand.

One of the first things I remember thinking about when I came out of my coma was about the Bible. We have this Bible, but we do not understand it. We are so close to understanding it, but we just are not there yet.

It is like you must be like a child to understand it. Because we are all so stuck in our own ways of thinking we do not open ourselves up to understanding even the simplest of things.

We think we already know, but we do not. In Genesis, the beginning of the Bible it says God put Adam and Eve on Earth to do what? "replenish (replenish) the Earth" RE meaning that Earth has already been populated before.

This is not the first time this Earth was inhabited. I have news for you this is not even the second, third or fourth time. Earth has been around for billions of years and if you think about it, it would be crazy to believe that we are the first humanoids here.

On this planet there have been many other versions of varied species and there has been many other versions of humanoids. Big one's small ones all diverse kinds of humanoids. Humanoids are not the only intelligent species to have ever lived or that is alive.

Look at the great pyramids of Egypt, some of the pictures engraved are interesting. Men with bird heads. Yes, that does sound hard to believe but if you came from a different planet and never seen an elephant or a giraffe before wouldn't you think that they were strange looking animals? You would, and they are strange looking. But they adapted to their environment so that they could survive just like millions of other species in our universe did.

There are countless species we have left to someday learn about and experience here and throughout the entire universe.

I mentioned before when we die or transform at the end of our life here on Earth, we go to the spirit world and some of us may be given a choice; we can come back here or start over. I do know that we will go to the next phase of our existence that we need to go to, that will best serve the learning needs that we have.

When we die or I should say our spirit leaves our bodies most of us choose not to fight going to the spirit world but some of us do and they remain here on Earth but in a different dimension.

They are here but most of us cannot see them. Sometimes they can manifest themselves to us by absorbing energy and then we can see them. Some of us are given a gift and can see them. I believe that we could all see them if we just knew how to use more of our brain.

There are many reasons why people do not follow the light and go to the spirit world. One is they may be attached to their home or another physical object. I know that if I worked hard my entire life and was able to build a beautiful home or have wonderful things, I would not be in a big hurry to leave it myself.

That is why if you focus on the things that you can take with you after physical death instead of things that you cannot take with you, you will be a much happier person. Knowledge and wisdom, education and experience and good karma is what you want. All that stuff that Jesus did was all good karma.

So, I am sure people are attached to their home or some other personal object. Some people are afraid to go to meet their maker because they have committed a sin that they have not taken the proper steps to resolve.

These steps or details I referred to earlier as repentance. To remove all the guilt, you may have acquired in your personal history.

There is a reason why we all have different personalities. Most of us have siblings and even though we all grow up in the exact same environment, we are much different from each other. The same family can raise one child who is successful and one child who is not so successful. Of, course that all depends on what you define success to be.

Your history can make an impact directly and indirectly in your present life.

In a past life someone can experience some kind of tragedy

and feelings from that can blead into and can influence your actions and emotions in this or another life.

If we have a litter of cats or dogs, they all have different personalities. Even though they all live in the same circumstances they do not all act the same. This can be because of the experiences that we have had in our past lives. They influence us even as far back as our pre-existence before we came here to Earth.

I know for example there are people that grow up thinking that they are gay because they are attracted to the same sex. I have heard many people tell me that they have always known that they liked the same gender. It is quite possible that they were the opposite sex in their past life, and they are still experiencing past emotions.

Learning is a part of growing and if we do not understand something, there is nothing wrong with that. That is natural because if we do not understand someone that does not make it wrong. We may all have had past lives and we will have many lives and or phases of existence in our future if we desire to. It is the only way we can learn, grow, and become powerful.

The more we learn the more power we have. Knowledge is power. "With great power comes great responsibility." (Spiderman) even though it was from Spiderman, does that mean it is not true? Of course not.

LEARNING HOW TO GROW

We can learn about our past lives and when you do you will start to understand why we act and think the way we do. That is why we have different personalities. I know two men, one has plenty of money but is very greedy and always wants more, so much he has even stolen from his siblings.

The other brother has no money but if he had a dollar, he would not hesitate to share it with others. The same upbringing but different personalities. Different personalities because of the different experiences in their past. Which brother do you believe is the successful one?

The one with the money or the one that will always help you if it is possible?

Is wealth the most important thing? I do not believe so. Gratification can make you feel good and money cannot buy gratification. It is something you do, what you do is who we are.

Take the time to do something good every day for someone you do not know for just one week and you will feel it yourself. Try it and you will see how good you will feel. Let good karma guide you down the pathway of your desires. The only thing you have control of in your life is your actions.

Your actions control what phase of existence you will experience next, good, or bad.

We can only go from one phase of existence to another the way we know how. We cannot go to a different phase of existence other than the ones we have already been in without learning or earning how to advance to a new phase of existence.

We may continue to have one life after another here on Earth or other planets until we have learned what we need to learn, to advance.

Some of us only needed one life here on Earth to learn what we need to learn but there are many of us that keep coming back because we must be slow learners or we just have not been in the right circumstances to learn what we need to learn.

We will all eventually learn what we need to learn then move according to our desires. To me, God is many things not just Extraterrestrial Eternal God, Father in Heaven and all-powerful creator and all-knowing God, and most of all the great collective.

Everting that has ever been learned or will be learned will be in the great collective we call God. The stronger and more powerful we become the more powerful we make him.

He has paved the way for us to have eternal life, it is a part of the plan. I believe that God was once like we are now, and we will have the opportunity someday to be like a God.

COMMITMENT AND
BEING COMMITTED

I used to have the joke for every occasion. If I got a couple beers in me, I could come up with a joke about anything. I had so many of my friends literally begging me to get into being a standup comedian. I think that it was pretty much during my drinking years I was the funniest, but maybe it was just the booze that made things seem funnier than they really were.

Tell me if you think this joke is funny. A guy was in the bar and he was telling this story about a car accident he was in. He says that in the accident he got his junk cut off. A lady speaks up and says, "you got your junk cut off in an accident?" and he said "yes, do you want to see it?" And she says, "Hell YA" So he reaches into his front pocket and pulls something out and says, "see here it is" She said, "that's not your junk, that's a cigar." He puts it back into his pocket and checks his back pocket and pulls out something and says, "see here it is" and a few people say "that's not your junk it's a cigar. One more time he reaches into a different pocket and pulls out another cigar and says, oops I must have smoked it.

I know I loved to joke a lot for most of my life. Even in

jail I tried to joke and prank. In jail there is this form you need to fill out if you want to find out if you have any added charges. You need to put your name and inmate number on it, and then the guards would investigate it for you.

There was this inmate a couple cells down from me I did not have any issues with him he just seemed like a good target. I filled this form out for him and you tell me, if it would have made you, mad or not.

Inmate Thompson 7682812 then check the box New Charges. You do not have to put anything else, but I put the charge as well. A few hours later the guard makes this announcement "attention Inmate Thompson 812 You do not have any new Barnyard Sodomy charges at this point, but I will keep an I out on that for you.

Everybody liked that one, especially the guards. He picked up a new nick name now he goes by Barney812.

I tried not to take credit for it, I even felt a little sorry for him. He did not have any problem in all probability, he knew that it was me. "What is up with that? I did not know that it was going to have quite the effect that it did. Well you know what they say about Hine sight, it is always 20 20 So sorry Barney812.

Now some of my jokes you might not get and that is probably a good thing. They finally let me out on ankle monitor if I worked for them for free. BS but at least I was somewhat free.

I had this cute Tiny toy poodle and he was so glad when I got home that he essentially never left my side again until he died in my arms a few years later. Anyway, his name was

Baby, a couple times a week I could bring him if it were ok with the guards.

We had to report in an office that is in the same area as the exit when you get released from jail. I set up this table so the inmates that were getting released would have to walk right into it. I sat in a chair and I would hold Baby until someone would come a long and I would tell them "stop hold out your hands this is a drug sniffing dog and we need to see if you are smuggling any drugs out of jail. They would hold out their hands and I would use Baby like a metal detector.

I waved him up and down and back and forth until I could see they were starting to get irritated. Then I would say he or she is clean, but you need to promise if you have any good drugs next time you must share them with us.

I was never serious and always kidding around. When I was married to my second wife, I went from not being a Dad to becoming a Grandpa. I was okay with that they were all great kids, Two 11 tear old twins a boy and a girl. We had two older sons high school age as well. I never had kids before and I loved playing around and joking with them, maybe too much. I had a lot of fun with them until it all fell apart.

It was a major reality check to have kids and I was not the best father I could have been. But they were fun. We took in their cousins because their Mom and Dad had some problems to work out. Those were great kids too.

Their Mother had cirrhosis of the liver and was told that if she ever drank again, she would die. Her kids lived with us for a while and then it was decided to let her move in as well.

She did great for a couple weeks and somehow, she got a bottle of Vodka. We found her laying on the floor in her own vomit. My dog then Jessy was liking up that mess before I could stop him. We rushed her to the hospital where they pumped her stomach out. It was gruesome to watch. Later that day we had to explain to her kids that she was not going to come home because she drank herself to death.

They were about 13 and 15 years old at that time. I look at Jessy and he is sick now; he was a black dog, but you could see his skin turned yellow. I rush him to the vet and after two blood transfusions he died. I was Very sad and pissed off. What can you do?

I know that joking around is fun but there comes a time when you need to be serious especially when you have kids. I will always treasure the memories I had singing and joking around with them, I do love kids.

My third wife, the fun was unquestionably over when I married her! I know you can go too far when joking around but, in that relationship, no joking around was tolerated at all. She was bipolar actually she was tripolar. If there is a tripolar she was undeniably it. I think she could make Benny Hill depressed.

So yes, I love women they are beautiful. I had six serious relationships worth mentioning, not all good. Anna my first love. Julie my first fiancé. Lonna my first wife. Suzie my first time I could be called a grandpa. My third wife the tripolar one. And my wife now, her name is Love.

So, I really do not have a problem with commitment, I have been committed several times. I did like that new girl "smell" though.

I also had two other girlfriends as well, Linda and Tracy.

When you have this many relationships go bad it becomes obvious it is not everyone else.

I spent a lot of time trying to find that perfect girl, that one true love but now I know that any of those girls could have been that perfect girl. But the common denominator was me.

I was the problem Marriage is not easy it takes two to make it work and with patience you can make most any marriage work. It takes patience and work on both sides, both partners in the marriage must try and have patience.

It is a partnership; you should always try to be on the side of your partner. Now if you disagree with your partner you need to step aside and work that out one on one; not in front of the kids or other people, one on one. The kids and everyone else need to know that you stand together.

MISTAKES CAN BE LESSONS

I may not be the best person on telling you advice on how to keep an everlasting marriage, but I am an expert on relationships that have failed.

After so many relationships that have not lasted, I know that it has not always been the other persons fault. After a while it is hard not to think that I am reason that these relationships all that went south.

I am a slow learner, but the most important thing is that eventually, I do learn.

I want to send this special message to all of you out there who a feeling bad for any reason, I feel your pain. I also want to tell you that I am sorry for anything that has hurt you. You a special person that deserves to be loved and you must begin with you. Love begins with you. I sincerely wish you all the happiness life can bring to you; everyone deserves to be happy.

There is a time to give up. If you or your children are being abused, physically or mentally the best thing to do is end that relationship.

If you are not happy now in a relationship, you will not be happy in the afterlife or next phase of existence in the same relationship.

If you commit to someone in your physical life or a past

life you can remain bonded in future lives and phases of existence. You do not want to spend eternity in a relationship that is abusive, and you do not deserve it. Everyone deserves to have eternal happiness.

If you do not find your soulmate in this life you could find them in the afterlife, spirit world or in your next life. Do not think that you will be alone forever if you do not find your soulmate in this life.

It is important to give yourself a chance to have happiness in this life but even more important is eternal happiness. Everyone will find their soul mate, you may already have your soul mate from a past life and not know it, which is why you have not found that special person in this life like me.

PAST MEMORIES AND SPIRIT GUIDES

There is so much to learn but we must learn everything in a sequence. We cannot learn some things before other things.

Like you must learn to crawl before you can learn to walk. I know that is just an example because we are not all the same and some of us do not ever crawl, they go straight to walking. Some people skip other things too in the great scheme of things.

We are not all the same and some of us are faster learners and advance rapidly through distinct phases faster than our counterparts.

I know growing up, there were times that I just knew things I should not have known, and I have had some things that were much easier to learn than other things.

We all do, there is a reason for that. We already have knowledge from past experiences and lives that we sometimes at random subconsciously access. Many memories come to us in the form of dreams.

Not only past memories come to us in our dreams, but we communicate with our spirit guides and guardian angels in our dreams as well.

Try sometime, write a letter and ask some questions. Read it out loud then to put it under your pillow and sleep on it for a while.

We all have Spirit guides and our spirit guides are most likely ancestors or loved ones from our past. They are without doubt ones who care about us and want to help us.

They influence our lives to do what they believe is the best for us and those around us. I believe that our spirit guides also communicate with other spirit guides and they work together to get us to do different things. I know of a time in which my spirit guide helped me to save a little girl from drowning.

I was having a swimming pool party for my daughter's 7th year birthday. There were a lot of patrons in that popular public pool that day. At full capacity there are a lot of things to try to be aware of for lifeguards. I see it could be easy to let something become unnoticed.

I felt like I was almost being dragged towards the other side of the pool and when I got there I looked down and there was one of my daughters friends Haven under the water unable to come up for air. I was able to reach down and grab her and pull her to safety. She coughed up some water and she seemed to be fine after that. She was in danger and she could have died.

We know it was either my spirit guide that made me go there or it could have been Haven's, or it was the Holy Ghost, but something helped me to save her. I know that I saved her life and I thank God for that. I know that we are influenced by our spirit guides or guardian angels and other things like the Holy Ghost.

They help us in our lives, we just need to be tuned into them. If we are tuned into God and our spirituality it will help us in our physical lives.

MANY ESCAPES

As I have been drafting this book, I have been looking back on all my experiences. I stood up to a charging bull, I was broadsided by a teenager in a speeding car, I fell through scaffolding that was on two flights of stairs and I almost starved to death in my own apartment. After that fall, I made it to bed but could not get out of bed nobody came over for a couple of days until Share Bear finally came over and checked up on me.

I was choked out and almost mugged, I was accidentally food poisoned. I was poisoned by gas and with drugs more than once; many times, I escaped death.

Another time I escaped death I was in the Philippines; I was almost kidnapped and beheaded.

THE LAST TIME I SEEN HER

After I got shot and had my near-death experience it took me 18 months to recover. I had this survivor's guilt and I was trying to deal with everything. I met this girl online it was Yahoo Singles. I put my profile on there and filled out some information and the next day I had some messages.

One beautiful island girl started messaging me. She was not in the criteria of what I was looking for, but I am feeling like I am getting too old to be picky. I did not think there was anything wrong with her, but she was twenty years younger than myself.

I got to know some other ladies there, but the same one would catch my eye. Her name was Love she was from the Philippines. We got to know each other over the next several months and I finally decided to go and meet her in person.

I was most definitely flattered she would have anything to do with me be honest. She was pretty and petite and acted so extremely sweet. It was not hard to fall for that. In fact, everyone said I was being catfished. Well I was not being catfished! well not that time. I did get catfished out of a few bucks though one time. Be careful of the scammers out there who prey nice people.

I flew to Manila to meet her there. Stepping off that plane

was like stepping into the twilight zone. Wow you get culture shock the first time you go to a place like that, what a trip. Everywhere you look there is a custom willies jeep or old US army jeeps all tricked out. I guess the US just left them after the war. But it is a beautiful place.

She was picture perfect. I do not think she pushed the scales much over 90 pounds soaking wet. We spent a week there and then flew to another island; Ca Ga Yan De Oro City was where her family lived.

We spent a week with her family and then flew back to Manila. As we left that airport, we were walking to a passenger pick up, I noticed there was a crowd waiting in line, I made my way over that direction to them. Just before I reached the pickup area a Taxi rolled up next to me and the driver jumps out. "Hey Sir, don't wait over there I'll take you!" Love and I looked at each other and decided to take him up on his offer. Bad decision.

After our luggage was loaded and we are sitting in the back seat, he drives off. "I'm going the Bay View Park Hotel" I tell him. Next, I see he is not going the right direction, "Hey where are you going? You are going the wrong way. I am thinking that he does not know that I know my way around there at that point. "I know I know but you need to call them first, you can call them in this building right here!" he yells!

He pulls over and says, "there is a phone in there you can see." In front of the car standing right in front of us I looked up and briefly seen her pointing her finger at a building. It was her my guardian angel I look, and I see four guys dragging an older couple into the building. I looked right back but she was gone, her purpose was to warn me, and she did. Now she was gone.

I reached over the front seat and put my arm around his face and neck. "I got a phone right here Mother Effer and I'm calling the cops!" "No! No! No! Problem Sir I'll Take you back I'm so sorry!" I am very street smart, and I could see we were getting set up to get robbed.

We got to our hotel it was over we did not get hurt so all was well I thought. Two weeks later I am back in the states and I see on world news that and older couple had been kidnapped in Manilla and held for ransom but eventually they got their heads cut off. It showed their picture and it was them.

That was the last time I seen her, but I know she is here watching over me and helping me when I need it.

I am struck with the thought, does everyone have so many experiences like I have had? Is this normal and am I just writing a book about a typical person? I am not sure, but I do think that it is important to mention one more thing.

That is, I believe that I have made so many bad decisions and gone down so many bad pathways that I should be a very unhappy and lonely person, but quite is the contrary.

I made many poor decisions and I survived probably for many reasons. My point is that forgiveness is for everyone not just a choice few, everyone. Some say God is love but I say God is for everyone. Everyone who wants to let him in. If I can change my life anyone can. If I could be forgiven anyone can. If I can help others anyone can. I want to start a revolution.

I want to get everyone together I can and do one good deed

after another to help those in need. We can all be guardian angels right here on Earth.

I want to reach out to everyone who has made bad decisions or feel an emptiness inside themselves that they cannot fill. It is not a good feeling to be empty inside or alone, but it does not have to be that way. It took me a long time to figure out how to make that emptiness go away but the important thing is I finally figured it out.

If someone like me can survive after all I have done, every bad road I went down and poor decision I have made, and now I finally feel good about myself and I don't feel alone, it is so important to get that out to everyone who might feel that emptiness so that they may overcome these kinds of feelings and live a happy life.

HELPING OTHERS
HELPS YOURSELF

One of the most important ways to overcome emptiness and loneliness or feelings of sadness and frustration is service. I know it does not make a lot of sense but when you are helping other people with their problems your problems just seem to go away or take care of themselves.

That is why I will mention a couple of different organizations to contact that I believe are exceptionally good organizations, but they are just suggestions.

You can do so much to improve your life by helping others just in your local neighborhood. I heard of a new resource just last night called Next-Door. This is a new resource that is a phone app. This can let you know about things going on in your own neighborhood. You can find out about your neighbors who may need some assistance, or they may also learn about you.

I am a big believer in Karma. You can create good and bad Karma in your life. If you create good Karma in your life it will affect the kind of life you will have in your next life. I know now since I had my near-death experience or I should say since I went to the spirit world, we all have more than one life here on Earth if we so desire. Creating good Karma will make your next life easier and more enjoyable. Creating bad Karma will make your next life harder.

You may have a nice life now but if you create bad Karma, like you treat your dog badly for example, in your next life you just may be a dog begging for table scraps. How would you like that? Not so nice.

If you have a nice life, say born into a well-to-do family if you want to have an even better next life, create good karma. To move up into your next phase of existence when this life is over, you must use your position to help others.

You cannot take your money into your next life or phase of existence, so it is best to use your position or resources to help those in need while you are here.

If there was a way to buy your way into heaven, that would be the way, but you must give with your heart. If you give your money without giving with your heart it will not help you as much. You must always want to in your heart to help others.

You do not need to have money or resources to help others, there is always a way to help people in need. The smallest of deeds to those who need it will create good Karma. You must not do things just to create good Karma, you must do charitable deeds with good intent.

Know that by doing honorable deeds you will have gratification and blessings because when you do virtuous deeds your problems will almost magically disappear. It is so amazing how helping others will help yourself if you do it sincerely.

LET US HELP OTHERS

I want to gather friends together and accomplish great deeds I want to build a water purification plant in Flint Michigan, because those people need it. I do not know them, but I would love to help them because I know they need it. I would love to meet someone who could help me with that project and so many other projects.

It would be wonderfully gratifying to be able to give something so simple but so important such as clean water to people.

I know that Flint is not the only place that needs a water purification center; I would love to build them in many places. Could you just imagine how much suffering you could eliminate by just giving people clean water to drink?

There are so many places in the world that need clean water like India and the Philippines, and I want to make it my responsibility to help people with clean water. Not to create good Karma but because they need it.

Many years of my life was wasted trying to build a bank account and collect belongings for myself and none of that stuff ever made me happy. I am so glad now that I figured out what is important, I am so glad that my life is not over, and I still have time to make a difference.

God helps those who help themselves. I have had so many experiences in my life, and I know I have not made the best decisions. I now have two college degrees and I have turned my life around. I am a happier person and all the emptiness and loneliness is gone.

I love helping others and I believe that the experiences I had growing up only better helps me help other kids who are having a tough time. I know I can relate to them more than most people can and I will always want to be there to help any kid who needs it.

I am just an Uber driver but I enjoy talking to my riders and getting to know them. I know that if I, after all I have been through can turn my life around and be happy person who loves life and helping others, I know that anyone can do it.

I went many years a hateful person, against police and I did drugs and dropped out of school. I know now that it was not easy but like I said, "if I can do it then anyone can."

My friend told me one time "for every good deed to you, perform two"

I believe that it is so important to help your fellow humankind. In some cases, more important than going to church every Sunday. If you want to learn about Jesus, or any other religion church is a suitable place to do it.

I hope it helps people become better and improve their lives. Just because you go to church though, does not guarantee that you will go to heaven. I believe it is also so important to be serving your fellow mankind.

I have a non-profit organization in the Philippines helping homeless children that live on the streets. They sleep on cardboard next to the buildings to keep dry from the rain and they are literally starving to death. My organization is Children International Unlimited.

It is though not to be confused with Children International which I do donate to. It is a great organization, I wanted to help children on a different level that they do.

They help children that live in poverty and most, from what I know live in small shacks for homes. The children I focus on are homeless. My Facebook page can be found by going to the Facebook home page search window and typing <u>Helping.homeless.children@Gmail.com</u> there you will see pictures of some of the children I help.

AGE OUT KIDS!

Thirty thousand kids age out of foster care every year in this country with little or no safety net at all. It is my life's mission to take in as many as I can. I want to start up an independent living program and trade school for them. I wish I could help them all. I believe that we could if we all got together. They are our greatest resource. They1 are our future and they are needing our help. Please help Age Out Kids as much as you can.

BE PASSIONATE

I believe that the single most important thing you can do in this life is to serve your fellow humankind. Do not just serve,

BE PASSIONATE!!!! Find something that you feel strongly about and be passionate about that. Give at least ten percent of your money to it if possible. After 365 days reevaluate your life and you will see that there have been opportunities fall into your lap which would not have otherwise. You will also see that your life is blessed.

In this chapter I decided to give some examples of organizations you can help.

I would love it if people donated to my Organization helping homeless children but if you find something you can be passionate about like I am, that is so important to give because you want to help others, not yourself.

I want to say my hats off to Alyssa Milano because of all her work in helping children in need. It would be a pleasure and a joy to someday meet her in person and tell her how great I think she is. So, it is for her that my first suggestion on organizations to support UNICEF. In one add she suggests donating 50 cents a day to help a needy child. That is less than a cup of coffee and a much better thing to buy. I hope that you can support UNICEF they are on my top golden list of organizations to support.

I would like to start a Golden Angel Society. You can join and become a Golden Angel and support all my top choices or pick one but know this if you support all these organizations you will be someone's hero and life saver. You can help to reduce suffering of an innocent child and there is no better thing to do in this life on Earth and in this phase of existence.

Speaking of a cheap cup of coffee, nowadays coffee is not so cheap. Just buying a caramel macchiato at some places is six or more dollars so I want to challenge them as well as all the big coffee places to a challenge.

Please donate 50 cents from every cup of coffee you sell and let us see who raises the most money for UNICEF. You have the power to save lives. Innocent children's lives and there is not a more important thing to save, please help them.

I also would love to tell Debbie Gibson thank you so much for all you do for Children International. She is also a wonderful and beautiful person that would be a day I could never forget if I met her.

This is my list of Golden Charities. Donate to all of them and you will be a Golden Angel. Choose any of them and you will still be a hero and a life saver and in my book an "angel."

Become a monthly Golden Angel or a onetime hero to

UNICEF 1800-367-5437 WWW.Unicefusa.org

Children International 1800-888-3089 WWW. Children.org

Saint Jude 1800-608-7836 WWW.Stjude.org/donate

Go Fund Me Helping Homeless Children

Thank you for your support, be passionate, treat every day as if it were your last and do not leave anything unsaid or undone.

Who are we? Where did we come from? Why are we here? Where do we go from here? Do I have a guardian angel? When I die, is it over? How can I live a happier life? **Did I ever have a past Life?** Will I have another life? Why do I feel the way I do? What is most important?

I got Shot 4 times and I was dead! While in a coma for ten days I began to access memories from a past life. When I woke up, I knew things that I did not know before. All these questions and many more I knew the answer to after I came back to Life.

Printed in the United States
By Bookmasters